THAT FIRST BITE

Rosalie - Rejoice in your Choice! - for that's where God is.

Love,
Mary Sullivan r.c.

CHANCE
OR
CHOICE?

A Working Guide
Empowering Choice For Those With
Eating Disorders

Rose Marie Dunphy
and
Mary Sullivan, r.c.

Jeremiah Press   Boca Raton, Florida

Excerpts from *Song of the Bird, One Minute Wisdom,* and *Sadhana* by Anthony de Mello used with permission of the publisher, Bantam, Doubleday, Dell Publishing Group, Inc.

Dedication

**To my husband, Jim, and our children
. . . Rose Marie Dunphy**

**To my Sullivan family, Cenacle family
and 12 Step family
. . . Mary Sullivan, r.c.**

ISBN   0-9631517-6-2

Available from:
**Compulsive Eaters Retreats
The Cenacle Retreat Center
1400 S. Dixie Highway
Lantana, Florida 33462**

Published by:
**Jeremiah Press
22921 Ironwedge Drive
Boca Raton, Florida 33433**

Table of Contents

PROLOGUE

You could say that four "f" words -- *fat, feelings, forgiveness, freedom* -- aptly describe the process set forth within these pages.

Yet, if you want to experience the transformation that is inherent in the journey from fat to freedom, then you'll want to read the pages slowly, at your own pace, absorbing all that you can identify with at one time. You'll want to enter into the exercises carefully and fully, reflecting on the insights and revelations the experiences may bring you.

These exercises work. They have been tried and proven successful in hundreds of retreats throughout the country. They have helped thousands of compulsive eaters to lead healthier, more satisfying lives.

Consistently, the exercises will bring you to the point where you can get in touch with your feelings. The choice to do so, however, will always remain yours. Trust your instincts not to take you further than you are ready to go.

Make this book an extension of you. Feel free to jot down any thoughts and feelings you have as you go along. In essence, you will be telling yourself *your* story. It will be the most interesting story you have ever heard.

There is a Zen saying that goes something like this: "When the pupil is ready, the teacher will come." This book is not meant to be your teacher but a guide. For when you are ready, you will see that pupil and teacher are one and the same.

Chapter 1
The Logic of Food

"I have a great family, a great husband, but when I'm into sugar, nothing really matters."

Once at a compulsive eaters retreat, a tall, dark, handsome, very overweight man whose name was Paul said, "I feel like I'm sitting on a fence. One side is food; the other, life. And I don't know which way to go." Burying his face in his hands, he burst into tears.

Most everyone can empathize with the dilemma Paul faces. The courage to verbalize it is in itself commendable, though he feels anything but courageous in doing so. Nor is Paul aware of just how lovable he is, expressing his deep, true feelings even though they hurt. He only sees his vulnerability and confusion.

You might ask, why does anyone have to choose between life and food? Can't they go hand in hand? When did the two become diametrically opposed? After all, isn't food part of life? Don't you need to eat in order to live?

Vivian, who attended the same retreat, put it this way: "I eat when I feel scared. I feel the food is going to take the fear away. If I feel lonely, the food will keep me company. If I feel excited or angry, the food will calm me down. Even if I feel fine, I eat to continue to feel fine. I'm not conscious of it, but I'm always hungry. For example, when I'm cold, I eat to get warm. When I'm hot, I eat to cool off. It never dawns upon me to put on a sweater or take one off instead. I realize it's so illogical. But it's a logic I grew up with."

A Sense of Security

For people who are compulsive eaters, food is a safety net. They automatically turn to food when they don't know where else to go. They crave food in order to deal with life. Somehow, food is going to take care of all their needs. They don't know they go to food because of their feelings. They don't realize that most of the time they eat to cover up their feelings.

Even after they have eaten, compulsive eaters are not full. There is no logic to it. Yet to them, food is the most logical thing to turn to again and again. They're hungry for it all the time. They have no idea what that hunger means or what it's for, but after they eat, they feel better. They're more relaxed. They're charged. Food becomes like the trusted friend who is welcome at all times of the day.

But in the course of time, food becomes an enemy. Sometimes slowly, sometimes suddenly, compulsive eaters begin to realize how dependent they are on food. They're addicted to it the way an alcoholic is to alcohol. And if they're interested enough to research the topic, they discover that, like the alcoholic, they too have a disease. Their disease is called compulsive eating.

At this point, read and complete the following exercise. Do not continue further in the chapter until you have first completed the exercise. Do this and all exercises that follow in the order that they appear and in the context of the chapter.

Approach the exercises as enjoyable and easy tasks. They are. Also, it's very helpful to take some processing time after each exercise. You may wish to do this alone or with a trusted other. Whether you spend one minute or several days is up to you.

Exercise 1

Close your eyes or leave them open but unfocused.

Imagine yourself without a food problem. Imagine that you don't binge or obsess over food. What would your life be like? Where would you be? What would you be doing, and with whom? How would you look, feel, and act? Write your thoughts below, letting your imagination run wild, and truly enjoying this exercise. If you need more room, continue on another piece of paper and later staple it to this page.

I would be living it to the fullest. In a comfortable, trim body; I'd be walking outdoors and feeling healthy and not hungry or craving food. I would look happy; trim and unafraid. I'd be with the man I love and making plans for our life together.

Before proceeding, gently say good-bye to that other you, that other life free from your food disorder. Now come back to the present.

That First Bite

Recognizing The Symptoms

Do you recall when you first were aware that you had a problem with food? One woman first realized it when she saw how each night she waited in bed, pretending to be asleep, until her husband fell totally asleep. Then, she'd quietly get up, walk into the kitchen, and eat to her heart's content. Later, she'd sneak back to bed and hope to God her husband hadn't noticed she was gone.

Another said it was when she began to throw food in the garbage and pour liquid soap over it. This way she wouldn't go back to the garbage to eat it.

"I knew I had a problem very early on as a child," said a third. There were different landmarks in my life that I can see as I look back. Perhaps it wasn't until I attended an OA meeting (OA stands for Overeaters Anonymous- a fellowship of individuals who, through shared experiences and mutual support, are recovering from compulsive overeating), that I realized my problem was with food. I used to think it was just with weight, even though I was eating in secret. So, on one level I must have known I had a problem with food. On another, I didn't."

Exercise 2

Draw a circle, like a sun and write the words "my food problem" inside it. Then draw lines like the rays of the sun. On each ray, write a word or phrase depicting a landmark, a stepping stone, an important event that occurred or step you took that you feel may have led to your present problem with food.

That First Bite

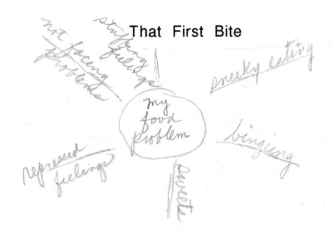

When you are finished, thank those rays for revealing a path that may have been hidden from you had you not looked back on it. Accept each ray as part of your past and bid them each farewell. For, in the past, they hold no more power over you. It's only when you allow them into the present, that they continue to control you. Come back to the present.

A Complex Disease

"Why is God allowing this to happen to me? Why doesn't God give me the strength to come out of it so that I can feel good about myself?" asked one compulsive eater.

"You've had fear. You've longed for love. You've longed for intimacy. So why aren't you overeating?" asked another of a friend who did not have a problem with food. "Why am I bingeing?" she lamented, not out of jealousy or vengeance but out of a real desire to know the reason for her disease. "I've yearned for the mother I never had because she died when I was five. You've longed for your father who left when you were twelve," she continued.

That First Bite

"Why am I compulsive about food and you're not?"

Like alcoholism, compulsive eating is a disease of escape, denial and isolation. Like alcoholism, it is multi-faceted, involving both the physiological and psychological aspects of your being. Your food disorder could be a direct result of the different hungers you have in life. But it may also be due in part to genetic or physiological factors. Your body may be predisposed to this disorder the way some people are predisposed to diabetes.

Janice Keller Phelps, M.D. and Allan E. Nourse, M.D., bear this out. In their book, *The Hidden Addiction And How To Get Free*, they state, "Addiction is a matter of biochemistry and genetics. . . . Addictiveness -- the capacity to become an addict to anything -- is a built-in physiological state, something you are born with."

Exercise 3

a) Draw a picture of yourself at age 7 at your family table. Don't be concerned about your artwork. The drawing has to be intelligible only to you. Stick figures or other simple symbols are perfectly all right.

b) What role did you play at the family table, e.g., eating, not eating, fighting, hiding, setting the table, serving the food, telling stories, crying, screaming, other? Answer below.

eating, serving listening

c) If there was an adult in your home at that time who had an eating disorder, how much of their communication or relationship with you was done through food? Describe below.

don't remember anyone,

Now come back to the present to look at your life today.

Exercise 4
a) Draw a picture of yourself as an adult at your present family table.

b) What role do you now play at the family table, e.g., eating, not eating, fighting, correcting, setting the table, serving the food, "pushing" the food on others, telling stories, hiding, crying, screaming, other? Answer below.

eating, correcting, setting, serving" + pushing food.

c) How much of your communication and relationship with others is done through food by you who has the eating disorder? Describe below.

most of my communication is done through food.

Many people, at this point in the exercise, express feelings of hunger. Jot down what you are feeling right now.

Thirsty

Chapter 2
Your Feelings And You

"I hate the way I feel about myself."

Exercise 5

Before you go further, take a closer look at your drawings under Exercises 3 and 4 in the previous chapter. Do you notice anything now that you may not have noticed when you first drew them? Whatever that might be, write it below:

my figure of myself is lower than the others — low self esteem.

Hidden Clues

For many, these drawings very often contain hidden clues. In reviewing them, the clues become obvious and provide signs that can help you understand the development and possibly the origin of your food addiction. For example, through her drawings Vivian, the retreatant mentioned in Chapter One, found that she was the only one without feet at the table when she was a child. She saw in vivid terms how powerless she was to leave the table. Another zeroed in on her father's hand over a wine bottle. It clearly reflected his present addiction to alcohol which he denied.

Paul, also in Chapter One, was surprised to see that he had drawn only himself at the table even though he had brothers and sisters. He realized that his focus was always on food because it served as a distraction or escape from the screaming and fighting that went on in his house. A woman recalled a strong need to keep quiet at the table. She had drawn herself with food in her mouth. Why? She couldn't argue back if she kept eating. Another man's picture was of someone standing and eating. He remarked that he never sits down at the table to eat. He usually eats alone, on the run, standing up in the kitchen somewhere. He recalled that his mother was a cook for a boarding school and he and his siblings could only eat while following her around in the kitchen. This was the only connection he had with his mother who worked all the time. His eating pattern was set at this time.

Exercise 6
What do your clues tell you? Answer below:

My whole life centered around food on the dining room table.

The Ability To Feel and Express Emotions
Compulsive eaters, like everyone else, undergo all the human emotions such as joy, fear, excitement, anger, resentment, pleasure, grief, helplessness, experiencing love and care, and feeling abandoned or rejected at one time or other in their lives. But compulsive eaters are unable to feel and express these emotions as easily as the general population. Instead, they block them out, shut them

down, negating their very existence.

"I hated my body even as a little kid," said one woman at a retreat for compulsive eaters. "When my mother and I went shopping for my clothes, I always made sure they had sleeves. If not, I made my mother sew them on to hide the fat on my arms."

"I was so self-conscious about being flat-chested that clothes shopping was a torture for me. I never bought brightly colored clothes because people would notice me. I even cut my hair short so as not to have anything feminine about me," said another.

"I have not wanted to remember my father who died six years ago," said one man. "It hurts too much and I don't like the anger that seems to come, so I stuff it."

"Every now and then I think of why my parents had me," said another. "Would they have wanted a house or car instead? But what does this have to do with my eating disorder?"

Perhaps a great deal. Test results by scientists are beginning to show that lack of emotion and addiction are somewhat related. An article in the April 1989 issue of *BRAIN/MIND BULLETIN* reports that recent studies by Polish researchers support this hypothesis. The article goes on to suggest further that the absence of emotion, a condition called alexithymic, is more likely a cause than a result of the addiction.

Feelings About God
This inability to feel or express emotions is not

just limited to feelings about themselves or other people. It also extends to how they feel about God. Some express total devotion to God. "God is the only one I can trust," said one man.

While for others the antithesis is true. "How can I trust God whom I don't see, when I don't trust others whom I do see?" said another.

Some are really angry with God because they feel God has cursed them with an illness. "My relationship with God is up and down like my weight," said one woman.

"I feel totally abandoned by God. God has never been there for me," said another.

Others simply don't look at God. They ignore God just as they ignore their weight or their addiction. "I have no problems with God. Everything is fine between me and God," said one woman.

Some hunger for God and if they eat enough food, they feel the hunger will be satisfied. They say there's a hole inside them which they try to fill with food. They're not consciously aware that it's really a God-hole they need to fill. "God has been answering my prayers in tiny little chips," said one compulsive eater.

Speaking in Codes

Feelings must be communicated somehow. When you don't communicate them verbally, they are communicated through your body. One compulsive eater shared the fact that when she is angry with her husband, she eats a pound of chocolate chip cookies. Others have said that they slam doors, put out the garbage, or dose out the "silent treatment."

Some eat in secret, or binge on certain foods, or purge, or stop eating altogether. Sometimes a whole system of eating certain foods to express certain feelings develops. There are people who say they eat carrots because they are crunchy and it expresses anger for them. Others will eat soft, smooth foods such as ice cream or jello when they feel shapeless and "blah." Compulsive eaters are notorious for using codes to express how they feel.

"Oh, do I have codes!" said one person. What are your codes?

Exercise 7

a) What do you do when you're mad?

eat + become sarcastic

b) What do you do when you're sad?

eat and cry

c) What do you do when you're glad?

eat

d) What do you do when you feel guilty or "bad"?

eat

Uncovering Your Feelings

"One of the things I never knew before I went to OA meetings was that I eat to cover up my feelings," said a compulsive eater. "I never felt my rage. I would feel afraid, but I didn't realize I ate to quiet the fear, to still it."

If you're angry, food covers the anger like a thick blanket of new-fallen snow. If you're anxious or afraid, food acts like fog to block out what you're afraid of or anxious about. If you're sad, food, like a tranquilizer, deadens the pain. When you feel guilty, food lifts the burden. Even when you're happy, food controls the pleasure so that you can handle it better.

Because some of their feelings are too painful and overwhelming, many compulsive eaters don't want to deal with them. Some totally deny their feelings. "I'm fine," they say. "It doesn't bother me." "My husband loves me." "I have a perfect home." "Everything is wonderful."

Finally you reach a point where, as one person put it, "I don't know how to identify my feelings." Food covers up not only the original feeling, but the secondary feeling as well, the one that tells you how you feel about having the original feeling in the first place. By now there's layer upon layer building up like barnacles on a rock, and like the rock, you're deteriorating underneath. Only you don't see it.

But the body does not lie. It sees and hears and feels everything. Feelings are always real, even when the perception of reality that brings on that feeling is not.

By nature, feelings need and want to be expressed. According to David Viscott, author of *The Language of Feelings*, trying to control feelings merely reshapes the way they may appear. When you deny the direct expression of your feelings, your feelings will store themselves in your body and express themselves through fat or binges or purging. Such expression only serves to trigger and fuel your disease further.

"It was a long time before I realized the connection between food and my feelings," said a compulsive eater. "I definitely never saw that it covered up feelings like anger or sexual feelings. Putting the food down made me feel raw with my feelings. When I did not eat compulsively, there was no longer any buffer zone."

Direct Expression of Feelings

You can't express your feelings directly as long as you are compulsive about your food. When you are into the food, you're letting the food speak for you. So if you want to express your feelings directly, you must begin by putting down your trigger foods. Don't purge. If you're anorexic, make sure you eat appropriately.

Once you stop abusing the food, you are free to feel and to recognize what you are feeling. In this stage, you can put a name to your feelings and know what they are. However, a word of caution is needed here. It takes a long time for the substance -- food -- to lose its numbing effect so that you can accurately identify what you are feeling. But if you want this to happen, it will.

As you begin to identify your feelings, you can start learning how to express them directly and appropriately. The best time to express what you feel is close to the time that you feel it. This prevents the build-up of excess baggage.

Then, express your feelings as honestly as you can. Practice by writing your feelings down in a journal or sharing them with a person you trust. Having learned to do this in these safe environments, you can now begin to express your feelings in an unsafe environment.

For example, one compulsive eater ate a whole pizza each time he had a fight with his mother rather than tell her how he felt. Though the pizza alleviated the guilt, it didn't take it away. He still had to deal with guilt and the added weight as well. After years of repeating this behavior, one day he decided to tell his brother how he felt. Through his brother's simple act of listening, this compulsive eater was strong enough during the next argument to tell his mother what he was feeling instantly, honestly, and without the pizza.

Exercise 8
Choose a past situation in which you have indirectly expressed your feelings through the abuse of food. If this situation were to recur, how could you express how you feel more directly? Answer below.

When I see things unjustly rewarded, even if they are blunders.

Jot down below what you are feeling right now.

angry at Eric, Walter, for making fun of Tony, me, Eileen.

Chapter 3
The Importance of Honesty

*"I can't find that one person to tell
the truth to. I go to a psychiatrist and I can't tell the
psychiatrist the truth. I find that heavy."*

It's not easy to face your feelings. But when you don't express your feelings directly either to yourself or someone else, you're being dishonest. When you cover up your feelings, you're lying not only to yourself but also to others.

For some people, covering up their feelings is quite acceptable. They think it's perfectly okay because it doesn't affect anyone. But in fact, this kind of dishonesty affects them greatly, and not only them but others also.

Being dishonest with food, with your feelings, with yourself, with others all serve to trigger the disease. Judy Hollis, in her book *Fat Is A Family Affair* says in no uncertain terms, "You are as fat as you are dishonest."

Hiding The Evidence

To minimize how much they consume, many compulsive eaters often hide or camouflage the evidence. This way their actions don't seem as bad, or appear to be what they are. For example, some re-arrange cookies so that they don't look as if any have been eaten. Others hide food in the basement or eat in a darkened room so as not to be detected. Others may adjust the poundage on the scale, or fast for one day, or purge through laxatives.

"I pack my own bag from the supermarket and eat the contents on the way home," said Vivian. "Then I look for a garbage can to get rid of the evidence."

Harmless as these games may appear on the surface, they're like playing with matches. If there is one person you can't lie to, it's yourself. Deep down you always know the truth, and such deception creates more problems than it solves.

Exercise 9
What are some of the ways in which you hide or camouflage the evidence? Write that below.

Facing the Truth

"I work in a deli. The reflection in the milk case shows me who I am -- this tiny little head on a huge body," said one compulsive eater. It was as close to the truth as she could get.

How do you face the truth if you've spent many years blanketing it? How do you bypass your patterned behavior codes in order to speak and act directly? How do you signal to others that you want them to break through your codes so that they know what you are feeling and want to say?

Four communication skills that have proven successful promoting honesty are I-disclosure messages, I-response messages, I-confrontive messages, and I-preventive messages. The reason they are successful is that they help you communicate accurately. The names may sound formidable at first, but they're really quite simple to understand and practice. The more you practice them, the more you can create and maintain an honest environment for your feelings and actions.

I-Disclosure Messages

I-disclosure messages disclose to another what you feel, what you need, what you think, what you value, what you believe in. They are those things you say about yourself to others that they would not know unless you said it to them. They are a direct, clear expression of what's going on within a person.

People are not mind readers. If you have a frown on your face, those around you might interpret it as meaning that you are annoyed with them when it may very well be that you have a headache or are worried about your child or have some other concern. To keep the lines of communication clear and honest, it becomes important to articulate what's really going on inside you. For example, "I feel happy" or "I feel sad" or "I'm worried." They're simple things, but unless you say them, people around you will not know them. Other examples might be, "That phone call disturbed me", or "I'm being bothered by this heat. I wish it would cool off."

Sometimes the I-disclosure messages are not tied to the situation at hand but are part of your makeup or belief system that communicate your views or your feelings at different times. For example, you might say to someone, "I value life," "I believe in God," "I need help," "I think family is important," "I like to swim," or, "I like to read."

Practice a simple I-disclosure message right now.

Exercise 10
Disclose to this space one thing about yourself that is true right now, such as what you feel, believe, think, value, or need.

I-Response Messages

These are your replies to what someone else says to you. Here, you respond in such a way as to let others know that you accurately heard what they tried to convey. For example, after your friend has told you all the fun things he did on his vacation, you might comment, "That sounds to me as if you really enjoyed yourself." If another shares how upset she is over a fight with her child, spouse or parent, you might answer, "That sounds to me as if you're hurt," or "That sounds to me as if you're angry." You respond to what you've heard and somehow from what you say, the other person knows you have heard them. Practice some I-response messages below.

Exercise 11
Write a simple I-response message to the following statements that someone else has just said to you:
a) I just heard I'm getting a promotion next week.

b) I can't believe my parents are getting a divorce.

c) How could my boss accuse me of not doing my job well?

d) My kids are driving me crazy!

I-Preventive Messages
In these messages, you are letting others know a need you have in order to prevent something from happening to you. These are most often used with people who are significant in your life. For example, suppose your friend has invited you to dinner. In order to insure that the right foods are provided for you, you might say, "Thank you for inviting me to dinner tonight. Please know that I cannot eat anything with flour in it, so I ask that you not serve anything containing flour with my portion."

Or, if you've had a rough day at work and wouldn't be able to handle it if your children or spouse asked you to do something for them, you might say to the family, "I've had an especially hard day at work today. Please don't ask me to do anything extra tonight. It'll have to wait for another day."

Exercise 12
Practice an I-preventive message by choosing a significant person in your life and letting him or her know of a need you have. Write your I-preventive message below.

I-Confrontive Messages

These messages are "I" statements you make to others to tell them how you feel about something they do, and how it affects you. This situation usually occurs when you have a problem with a person. For example, "When you drink, you verbally abuse me and I feel lacking in dignity." Or, "When you stand over me as I talk on the telephone, I get the sense that you're monitoring every word I say. I feel that my privacy is taken away." Another might be, "Every time I tell you of a problem I have, you instantly give a solution and start to solve it. I don't feel heard or understood."

Exercise 13
Practice an I-confrontive message by choosing a

person with whom you have a problem. Tell that person what action of theirs it is that bothers you and how it affects you. Write your I-confrontive message below.

Staying Honest

For your own personal integrity and emotional stability, it's always best never to lie. Yet, telling the truth at all times can sometimes present a dilemma. It did for Vivian. "I just know when I return from this retreat, my neighbor will ask me where I've been all weekend. I don't want to tell her. It's none of her business and she doesn't need to know," she said heatedly to the group. "I had already decided that I would make up something to tell her on the way home, but now that you are saying to be honest at all times, I don't know what to do," she continued.

Vivian has a very good point. There are some people that don't need to know, nor would you wish them to know, information about you or feelings you may have. These are components of your vulnerability and your privacy that need to be protected at different times and from different people. But the goal of being honest at all times still stands, for when you are dishonest in some things, you slowly begin to be dishonest in others. How do you resolve this thorny issue?

There are several approaches you can take that will keep you honest and intact and still preserve your confidentiality. When someone asks for information that you don't want to divulge, for example, you can always say, " I don't care to share that information, thank you," or "I'd rather not say," or, "It's rather personal." But if such answers are awkward for you, you can choose one non-consequential thing that's true about the information and divulge only that. For example, the woman above could say, "I spent the weekend with friends." That certainly was true since, by Sunday, most people were quite friendly. Or she could name the city or town she was in, for example, "I was in New York." If you can anticipate the question and practice what your response will be, you'll feel less threatened and more in control.

So often people, like Vivian, don't realize the dishonesty that can exist in their lives. Becoming aware of it and trying to live a life that is honest makes everyone healthier and happier.

Exercise 14
Choose something that you don't want someone to know, e.g. that you are reading this book, that you go to OA meetings, that you don't eat certain foods, etc. What truthful but not threatening response could you give someone if he or she asked you about it? Write that below.

Jot down what you are feeling right now.

Chapter 4
Control Games People Play

"I say to everyone, 'Catch me if you can.'"

Because they feel out of control, compulsive eaters try to control through their addiction. As such, they end up playing games -- games with their food, their weight, and their appearance.

Games People Play With Food
"Game playing is my gift and curse," said Paul. "I've eaten out of the garbage as well as at the table. I've eaten for others, in spite of others, to stay asleep, awake, to decide to laugh or cry, when in love or out of love. I've lied, cheated and stolen in order to eat. I've used people and twisted my relationship with others in order to eat. Food has always been my fellow gamesman, my insulator, my God."

"I use food as a reward," said Vivian. "When I do something good at work or for my family, I stash away my favorite foods in parts of the refrigerator where others won't find them so that I can have them later."

"Someone called me a double dipper once because I have to eat two of everything," said another compulsive eater. "If I have one banana, I have to have a second one right after. If I have an ice cream cone, I must follow it with another. I can't eat one candy bar. It's got to be two."

People with eating disorders play endless

games with food. Some eat hiding in bathrooms, basements, closets, or with the lights off so that they won't be seen. Sometimes, these games backfire. "Once, as I was eating a turkey club sandwich in the bathroom, I suddenly began to choke," said a compulsive eater. "I felt buried within myself, unable to breathe. Finally, after what seemed like an eternity, my husband heard some of my muffled sounds and gasps for air. He had to perform the Heimlich maneuver to dislodge the food. He was good to me. When I could finally breathe free, all he said was, 'Are you OK?'"

Others run the water, the blender, or vacuum cleaner so they won't be heard chewing. Some people never eat breakfast, or compulsively eat that which they think is "legal" such as ten fruits a day or nine helpings of vegetables. Others, especially bulimics, overdose on high-fiber foods because they tell themselves these foods are nutritious and aid the body's natural process of elimination.

When confronted as to where the food left over from dinner went, some say that the dog ate it, or it was thrown in the garbage. Unfortunately, these lies become distorted until compulsive eaters believe they are the truth.

Exercise 15
What are some of the games you play with food? List them below:

OPERATING INSTRUCTIONS

Enjoy your new quartz Folding Travel Alarm Clock !

FEATURES
- Durable reinforced plastic case
- Fold-over cover protects the clock face and folds back to provide a stand for your clock
- Glow-in-the dark hands.
- Accurate quartz alarm.
- "AA" battery included.

SETTING YOUR CLOCK

Step 1 : Inserting the battery
- Open the battery door located on the back of the clock.
- Follow diagram at bottom of battery compartment.
- Insert the battery, "+" side first, then press the "-" side in place.

Step 2 : Setting the time
- Using your thumb, apply light pressure and rotate the Time Set Knob. Hour and Minute Hands will move. Knob can be rotated in either direction.

Step 3 : Setting the Alarm
- Using your thumb, apply light pressure and rotate the Alarm Set Knob. Alarm Set Hand will move. Knob can be rotated either direction.
  NOTE :   Alarm Set Hand will not pass the Hour Hand when the Alarm Set Hand is moving in the clockwise direction.
- The Alarm On/Off switch must be in the "On" position for the alarm to sound.

Step 4 : Turning the alarm off
- Move the Alarm On/Off switch to "Off" position.

FRONT VIEW

BACK VIEW

CUSTOMER SERVICE- WARRANTY INFORMATION, QUESTIONS REGARDING YOUR CLOCK, COMMENTS
Your satisfaction is our biggest concern.
If you have any questions please call 1-800-473-8288 (8 30am to 5:00pm CST)

Games People Play With Weight

For women, one of the most common games played is the 'pregnancy prance.' One recently said, "I still use giving birth as my excuse for the extra weight. My son is fourteen years old."

Many games revolve around the scale. Some stand on the scale with one foot off. Others weigh themselves when the batteries of the scale are wearing down. "Then, I weigh myself all day long," said a compulsive eater. Others weigh themselves before breakfast and after breakfast, with their clothes on and with them off, with their jewelry on and with it off.

"I pretend the scale doesn't exist," said Vivian. Some people regard their weight as classified material never to be divulged. Others outright lie.

Exercise 16
What are some of the games you play with weight? List them below.

Games People Play With Appearance

People with eating disorders are extremely sensitive about how they look. This includes men as well as women. Feeling powerless about their appearance, they often invent ways to camouflage it. "I train myself to look in mirrors," revealed one woman. "If I prepare, I know how to look and not see. But If I'm off guard, I'm shocked."

"I became very obsessive about how I look. Different mirrors give me different expressions," said another.

"I was always attracted to black and dark clothes."

"I look for others bigger than me and I say, 'Look how good I am.'"

"I hate photos. I make sure I'm never in them."

"In the past, I wore a caftan. Now with God's help, I can get into tent dresses."

"I never wear horizontal stripes. I wear solids rather than flowery prints."

"I never wear anything form-fitting."

"I never wear jeans."

"I never wear shorts."

"So much of my time and energy is spent on calculating what to wear."

Exercise 17
What games do you play with your appearance? List them below.

Putting A "Game" Name On The Addiction

The rituals that people play with food, weight or their appearance produce and define the kind of "game" they play. The game creates the illusion of control. Games are not only necessary to face the day, but also charge the players with new-found energy. They provide welcome amusement. This was evident at a recent compulsive eaters retreat. Participants were asked, "If you had to give your addiction a 'game' name, what would it be?" They answered with relish and gusto. Here are some of their replies:

* Russian Roulette
* Never-Ending Circle
* Hide & Seek
* Who Do You Trust?
* Sorry
* This Little Piggy
* Catch Me If You Can
* What You See Is What You Get
* Monopoly
* Jeopardy
* Blow Up Or Throw Up
* Crazy Ates

Exercise 18

If you had to give your addiction a "game" name, what would it be? You can give it more than one name.

Rules That Your Addiction Is
Making You Play By

All games demand rules to keep the game operative and challenging. Though compulsive eaters have a sense of and get a kick from the games they play, they are often surprised to hear that their addiction imposes rules on them. But upon reflection, they find out this is true. Almost all of these rules are negative and self-demeaning. They further serve to isolate the person and to decrease self-confidence and morale. Like a vicious cycle, the rules insure that the addiction stays alive and active. The more you play the game, the more engrained and rigid the rules become. The more engrained and rigid the rules become, the stronger the game's addiction becomes.

Here are some of the rules addictions make people play by:

* Any good feelings you have are wrong.
* Don't accept compliments.
* Expect nothing because you're not worthy.
* Don't trust tomorrow.
* Never relax.
* Leave me alone.
* Peace at any price.
* Don't make waves.
* Only one player needed.

Exercise 19

What rule or rules is your addiction making you play by? List them below.

The Price You Pay

At compulsive eaters retreats, participants have shared the price they pay for playing these control games. They experience a loss of self-esteem -- "I am garbage." They experience shame --"I feel so guilty, so low." They experience self-hate --"How awful I must be to do this." They experience unworthiness -- "I'm unlovable." They experience a profound sense of estrangement from themselves -- "I go outside and people call me a sloppy pig." They fear intimacy -- "How can I let them know who I am?" They sense the imminence of insanity -- "I'm going crazy." They become physically disabled with bronchitis, pneumonia, rashes, infections, diabetes, high blood pressure, or other ailments. Some even die.

Exercise 20
What price are you presently paying for your eating disorder? Write that below.

Jot down what you are feeling right now.

Chapter 5
When You Control Others

"I turn my daughter away in order to eat.
I tell her I'll be there in a little bit.
But I don't go."

Through their food addiction, compulsive eaters are controlling others.

"Who? Me? Control others? My food problem affects only me!" insisted Paul when presented with this concept. This is the fallacy many compulsive eaters swear by. It's only when they begin their recovery that the veil of their disease is lifted from their eyes.

"I realize now what I'm doing to my family. My son is a yo-yo with his weight," said one compulsive eater who is in recovery.

"My daughter mirrors me," said another. "She's overeating, bingeing, isolating."

When you exert control through your food addiction, a number of unanswered issues emerge. They affect the entire family, both immediate and extended, as well as friends and co-workers.

The Question of Attention

At the dinner table, compulsive eaters control by monopolizing everyone's attention. When a person is overeating or undereating, all of a sudden, the focus of attention revolves around him or her, sometimes to the detriment of others who may have a pressing problem to discuss or an experience to relate. Invariably, the conversation is food-related.

"My wife watches and comments about everything I put in my mouth," said one compulsive eater.

"My husband is always yelling at me to eat, eat, eat," said another. "The whole family thinks I should put on more weight."

"Now that I'm off my diet, everyone questions my health. You'd think they felt afraid I'd have a heart attack or something," said one father with a sheepish grin.

Deep down in their gut, compulsive eaters know this kind of attention isn't healthy. But they don't know how to communicate their needs any other way. As far as they are concerned, attention through food is better than none. They are so afraid they'll get no attention at all, that they're willing to settle for this.

Exercise 21

a) What attention are you seeking through food? Write that below.

b) Using the communication skills learned in Chapter 3, how can you communicate this need in a more appropriate way? Write that below.

The Question Of Shame

People are often ashamed of their compulsive eater spouse. They cut down on inviting their spouse to accompany them to business functions. They're reluctant to bring business colleagues home. They're ashamed to go out together socially with friends, neighbors and extended family.

"We hardly go out anymore. And we always attended so many business and social events with friends and co-workers," said one compulsive eater in apparent bewilderment.

Children of compulsive eaters feel the same way as the spouses. Rather than have friends over after school or on weekends, they go to their friends' houses instead. "It's more fun there," they say, hiding their shame and increasing their guilt.

Compulsive eaters are not immune to their own shame and disgust. They don't like the way they look or how much weight they have gained or lost. They become depressed with a closet-full of clothes that no longer fits. They feel lethargic and powerless to control their food urges. As much as they mind missed opportunities, they often use their weight as an excuse not to participate, and the status quo is perpetuated. "Go without me, dear. Tell them I'm not feeling quite right," said one compulsive eater to his wife.

"Oh I'm not up to company tonight, honey," said another.

"Go over your friend's house, angel. You always love it there," a mother says repeatedly to her child. Sometimes consciously aware of the deception and sometimes not, the mother knows she wants to eat alone, with abandon, and in the open without any restraints.

Exercise 22
a) Describe a time when, because of your food addiction, you noticed a member of your family experience shame. Write that below.

b) Describe a time when because of your food addiction, you have felt ashamed to go out or have company. Write that below.

The Question Of Holidays And Social Events
Compulsive eaters often control the makeup and location of family celebrations. As their disease progresses, more and more, compulsive eaters want their parents and other relatives to come to their house for the holidays. Why? "I get the leftovers," confessed one woman. "And in preparing the food," she added, "I can eat as I cook it."

"When I go to someone else's home, I have to dress up," said Vivian. "Since none of my good clothes are comfortable any more, what can I possibly wear?"

"I need my own bathroom," said a bulimic. "If I'm in someone else's house, I can't be as free to exit during the meal."

With co-workers or friends, the compulsive eater is usually the one who determines what the social occasion will be and how it is going to be celebrated. He or she will pick the restaurant or make sure there's food served at a party, just the way an alcoholic would make sure there are drinks available. A compulsive eater is also the person who usually assumes the responsibility of collecting any necessary money for parties and gifts. He or she can then make sure food is part of the package.

Exercise 23
Where are your holidays spent? Why? Who makes the decisions or assumes the responsibility for most of the events that take place within your family or at work? Answer below.

The Question Of Fights
Many compulsive eaters deliberately provoke fights with their families. A retreatant related this story. When she had to go somewhere such as

Thanksgiving dinner with the relatives, on the way out the door, she invariably found something to fight over. For example, she'd say she just remembered a previous appointment or, all of a sudden, she didn't feel well enough to go. Her husband and children, often caught by surprise, would be enraged by these last minute tactics. Harsh words would be uttered. In the end, she would be so hurt, that she felt she could not be in the same car with them and told them so. The husband and children left without her, but were weighed down with the anger, guilt, and perceived responsibility for the fight.

"I purposely provoked my husband and children into going without me so that I could stay at home alone. I needed to be free to eat all day, at my own pace," she explained. "I also didn't want to face any relatives about my weight. The fight was the only legitimate way I could do it. But, it always left me with guilt because I knew I'd set it up."

Exercise 24
Can you think of a time when you provoked a fight to serve your eating disorder? Describe that below.

The Question Of Food Shopping

On the surface, compulsive eaters do not believe they control what foods are brought into the house. "I buy oreos because the children love them," said one woman. "But, in essence, I'm the one that can't put them down."

"I still say I'm getting the groceries for my kids," said another. "But my kids are grown, married, and out of the house. They rarely visit anymore."

"At the store, I cater to the dictates of my family," said a third. "Yet I know, I own a controlling interest in what I buy."

Diets are another issue that can become a tug-of-war with the family. When the compulsive eater is on a diet, he or she will keep certain foods out of the house as a form of control. "'You have no right to bring that in. You know I'm on a diet and can't have that,' I tell them. But what I really mean is, 'You can't have it because I can't have it.'"

Exercise 25
How do you exercise control with the food that's brought into the house? Describe that below.

The Question Of Money
Finances are another big issue. Of course the food budget increases in a household with a compulsive eater. But often there are other, hidden costs involved. "I was spending between $12 and $15 a day on fast foods," said one man. When he multiplied this figure by five days, it became $75 per week. Times four weeks, it was $300 a month. For the year, he discovered it amounted to $3600! "I realized that my food-fix was not inexpensive," he said.

Then there are the costs of the countless diets from which compulsive eaters go on and off. Physicals before the diets and medicine and doctor visits for illnesses caused by the disease compound the financial burden.

Exercise 26
How much money would you save if you didn't have to feed your food problem? Compute that below.

The Question Of Responsibility

Many household chores do not get done when there's a compulsive eater in the house. Obese men can't mow the lawn because they become physically tired and out of breath pushing the lawn mower. Family members, not wanting to lose their husbands and fathers to heart attack deaths, will often take on the job or pay others to do it.

Women who stay at home to raise the children and keep house will often have little time and energy to do either when they support a food disorder.

"I let my little children do what they want during the day," said one woman. "It's great when they go to a friend's house to play."

"I sit all day in front of the T.V. Then when it's about 3 p.m., I start cleaning the house. When my family comes home from school and work, they think I've been working hard all day," said another. And to relieve the mother and finish tasks on time, children will often help or take on the job completely once home from school.

Exercise 27

What responsibilities are being neglected because of your eating disorder? Describe that below.

The Question Of Mood And Mood Swings

Many times, compulsive eaters will allow or not allow things to happen in the house depending upon their mood of the day. This can be a direct result of "uncomfortable" feelings such as shame or guilt that they are wrestling with. Or it may be due to the after-effects of sugar or other food binges or withdrawal symptoms. Compulsive eaters can often create such a climate of violence that they are inapproachable. At such times, family members never know what to expect or when it's a good time to be with the person.

"There's a lot of punishment and reward in my house," revealed one woman. "When I'm feeling good about myself, I'm good to the children. But when I'm feeling low, then I ground them for the slightest thing. I remove telephone privileges or subject my husband to the silent treatment."

"Sometimes, I scream at the kids simply for walking into the room. I was planning to eat alone and undisturbed. By coming in, they've upset my plans," said one man.

"My kids are in fear and trembling the minute I put my foot through the door," said another.

Yet at other times, compulsive eaters are strictly people-pleasers. They can't do enough for their family. "How can they say anything bad about me when I'm nice to them?" explained a compulsive eater. "And, for a while at least, I think they'll forget about my disease."

41

Exercise 28
Choose one incident in which your mood or mood swings affected your family's behavior or freedom. Describe that below.

The Question Of House Rules
Sometimes compulsive eaters set up silent but understood rules that everyone in their household must abide by. These rules keep the focus off the addiction so the addiction can be denied. Here are some that were shared at a recent retreat.

* Don't talk to me about my weight.
* Don't tell me what to do.
* Don't rush me.
* I can do it myself.
* I'll let you know when I want advice.
* No communication allowed.
* Read my mind.

Exercise 29
What are some of the house rules you impose on your family as a result of trying to control them because of your eating disorder? List them below.

The Question Of God
"Even though I grew up in a religious

environment, I've stopped praying and going to Church. What's the use? God is never there when I need him," said one man.

"I don't let a day go by without asking for God's help in losing weight and in getting my life back together again. I tell God as soon as he does his part in changing my life around, I'll do mine," said another.

"I can't trust God because I don't trust myself," said one woman.

"I make promises to myself and God about food: -- just this once, -- just for today, -- just for this vacation, -- I'll start my diet tomorrow. I delude myself," said another.

"God never says anything good to me," said Vivian.

Because compulsive eaters feel so out of control of their disease and their lives, they often see God in the same light. They blame God for their failures and lack of control. They conclude that if their situation is so futile, so must be God's ability to care for them.

In fact, compulsive eaters don't trust God as the one in charge of the world. As far as they're concerned, God is not running the show properly. God doesn't do things right, so they must take charge and do it themselves. They must take control over what God should be doing or is doing wrong. It's a whole way of playing games with God, like, "I can do it better than God."

Jot down what you are feeling right now.

Chapter 6
When Others Control You

"There's a lot of controlling going on in my house."

Behind every compulsive eater you'll find people who think they can control the food abuse. Because of their function in the life of the compulsive eater, these controllers are referred to as enablers or co-dependents. Co-dependents are so intertwined with the compulsive eater that their mission in life becomes to cure the compulsive eater. But in actuality, they are partners in keeping the disease alive.

"The first thing my future mother-in-law did when I first met her was to take away the candy her son and I had in our hands. 'You don't need that,' she said. Now that we are married, she continues to manipulate us. She brings out the dessert and when we reach to take it, she calls us fat."

The Co-Dependents In Your Life

Statistics show that for every compulsive eater there are about fifteen to twenty co-dependent accomplices. Somehow, these people seem to have an inappropriate hold on the compulsive eater. The co-dependent might be a closet alcoholic who is able to mask his or her excessive drinking by being with a compulsive eater. It might be someone who finds security in exerting power and control over another. It could also be someone who is acting out a role learned and played since childhood, such as caretaker or scapegoat. Whatever the reason, for as long as the compulsive eater is willing, that inappropriate hold will be operative in the compulsive eater's life.

"The biggest controller in my life has been my mother," said one compulsive eater. "She'd say to me, 'Why don't you lose weight like I do?' Yet, she was the one that cooked for me. Now my mother has been dead for five years and I tell myself I'm fat because she's dead."

Who are co-dependents? "They're my trigger people," said one man. "Those whom I can never please, those who cannot give me anything."

"They're people I'm attracted to, whom I envy, exciting kinds of people," said one woman.

"People I see myself in, that have my weaknesses," said another.

"For me it's my brother," said a man. "I ate in reaction to his control and non-control. It was a no-win situation."

"I live with a bulimic," said another. "I eat when I witness her compulsion."

"At one time it was my sister, but now I've handed that control over to my husband," said one woman.

"My father is a compulsive eater in denial," said another. "I get involved with his crazy diets."

"Every member of my family on both sides is compulsive about something," said one compulsive eater.

"In my life, I feel I'm creating people who are

co-dependent on me," said another.

Exercise 30

Who are the co-dependents in your life, the people who have an inappropriate hold on you? Write some of their names below. You may use initials or code names. The important thing is that *you* know who they are.

How Co-Dependents Operate

The following questionnaire, adapted from *FAT IS A FAMILY AFFAIR* by J. Hollis will help you find out how your co-dependents have been behaving with you.

Exercise 31

Place a Y for YES or an N for NO next to each question.

_____	Do they force diets?
_____	Do they threaten to leave due to your weight?
_____	Do they check on your diet?
_____	Do they make promises based on the pounds you lose or gain?
_____	Do they throw food away so you won't find it?
_____	Have they excused your erratic, sometimes violent, mood swings

resulting from sugar binges?

_____ Do they change social activities so that you won't be tempted by the food served?

_____ Do they manipulate budgets to control spending on food and clothing?

_____ Do they purchase and promote eating the "right" foods?

_____ Do they promote gyms, health spas, exercise and miracle diets?

_____ Do they break into emotional tirades when they catch you bingeing?

_____ Are they constantly disappointed when they see you relapse?

_____ Are they embarassed by your appearance?

_____ Do they falsely console you when they are embarassed?

_____ Do they bribe with food?

_____ Do they talk about your body to you or others?

_____ Do they blame family situations on your weight or eating behavior?

_____ Does your eating disorder give them license to run away?

_____ Does your eating disorder give them license to stay?

_____ Do they subtly leave "helpful" literature around the house?

Four or more YES responses strongly suggest the presence of a co-dependent in your life.

Disguises Of Co-Dependents

If you are surprised at the results of the questionnaire in Exercise 31, there's a reason. Co-dependents live under a multitude of disguises. Very often, they play the role of rescuer, fixer, controller, or even the addicted one. "I ate everything in the refrigerator, so that my bulimic daughter wouldn't," said a co-dependent mother.

Sometimes, they change who they are and what they are feeling to please others. "I know my husband doesn't care for the movies much, but he'll go with me because he knows I don't like to go alone, and also to make sure I don't overload on popcorn."

They're overachievers who become almost superhuman. They'll clean the house, mow the lawn, take the dog to the vet, shop for the holiday gifts, bake five dozen cookies and more all in one day. Or they can be underachievers. All they do is fret, worry, and be depressed. Because they feel so burdened with the weight of others, they have no time or energy left for anything else.

Sometimes, they play the martyr or victim role. "After all I've done for you, what have I got to show for it?" At times they have such a grandiose air of control about them that they feel they can move mountains. But at other times, in order to accomplish their shoulds and shouldn'ts, they can bully others into doing as they say. "I had to lose fifteen pounds before my birthday," said a college student, "or my mother was going to cancel the party I'd planned with my friends."

Exercise 32
What kind of disguises do the co-dependents in your life take on? Describe.

Characteristics Of Co-Dependents

Ironically co-dependents suffer from the same problems as the person with the addictive disease. Why? Co-dependents identify with the person who is addicted. They build their whole lives around this person to the detriment of their own existence. Co-dependents are usually people who grew up in a dysfunctional family. As adults, whether consciously or unconsciously, they are often attracted to and choose partners or families who also do not function appropriately.

Like the addicted person, co-dependents tend to hide their feelings. They don't know how to express them. "How do I feel about it? What's there to say? Whatever makes my family happy makes me happy," said the wife of a compulsive eater.

They may seem happy on the outside, but inside they may be suffering from anxiety, fear, depression, and more. "Why do I feel like such a failure? I'm not the one with the disease!" said one man to a group of compulsive eaters.

Part of their conditioning is to respond more strongly to the input of others and the outside environment than to their own needs and inner experience, even to the point of denial. Because the delicate balance between emotional attachment and who they are as individuals becomes clouded, they often have difficulty making their lives work. "Why does everything have to fall on my shoulders?"

Like compulsive eaters, co-dependent counterparts have a low self-esteem. They never pat themselves on the back. They can't accept a compliment. Yet, they are overly dependent on others for approval and a sense of worth, and are quite possessive in their relationships. Others' needs and wants always come first. "If I don't do this, he (she) may not love me." It's never okay for them to make a mistake. Driven by compulsion, they can be perfectionists who are super-responsible at work and at home. But other times, they break under the pressure and may become super-irresponsible, put things off, and be unable to make decisions.

Two core issues for co-dependents are fear and shame. They fear being rejected and abandoned, so they must constantly prove themselves worthy to earn and warrant another's love and acceptance. Co-dependents also feel a personal sense of shame. They feel "less than". No matter what or how much they do for the other, it's never enough. They have to be the best they can, but they never can be good enough. Caught in this web, they are in a constant state of stress. Many suffer from migraines, colitis, hypertension and more. Co-dependency thus establishes itself as a disease.

Exercise 33
Choose one or more of the co-dependents in your

life. From what you know of them or their past, what need or needs is each working out of as they co-depend on you? Write that below.

When A Person Is Both Addicted And Co-Dependent

This situation is not only possible, but is also very common. "I'm a controller not with my daughter but with my son," said Paul. "I monitor what he eats. My father had the same situation with me. I'm doing what I learned as a child and I'm trying to pass the disease on. I hate it."

"I am both a compulsive eater and a co-dependent, so much so that I can't distinguish the two. I have *both diseases*," lamented another.

"I want to give up this control. I feel it's two steps forward and three back. I want to give my family more than I had," said a third.

Exercise 34
Are you a co-dependent? In what way and with whom? Describe below.

Jot down what you are feeling right now.

Chapter 7
The Paradox Of Control

"I only eat to stop tomorrow."

"I have been pretending for twenty-eight years," stated a business woman. "I'm in advertising, fulfill public speaking engagements and work on Madison Avenue. Yet it took me a full month before I could talk at an OA meeting. Then, to my surprise, this tiny voice came out." Such is the paradox of control.

A certain amount of control is necessary and even desirable in daily living. For example, it's important to run out of a burning building, or to do the wash when you've no more clothes left to wear. But when control is misplaced or does not relate to reality, then the consequences can be costly.

Reflecting on the issue of control, a compulsive eater shared, "I want to control so no one can hurt me." The outcome, she explained, is that she often refuses to face some of the events in her life. Food becomes her protective cover. And she thinks she is in total control. She, and not the event, now seems to be running the show.

The Faces Of Control

When your control does not acknowledge the reality of a situation or person, it's showing you its false face. It's only when your control addresses the reality of a situation or person, that you're seeing control's true face.

Let's examine this on a concrete level. Can you control the cars on the street or its drivers so that your child crosses safely? Of course not. What you can control is your response to the possible danger involved. Perhaps, you'll accompany the child while crossing. Or, if your child is old enough, you may decide to teach him or her how to cross alone. You can also regularly remind the child to look both ways before crossing. Do these insure the safety of your child? Hardly. But they do help promote it.

We'll carry this a step further. Suppose you can't deal with the uncertainty that your child might not make it safely across the street. After all, who is more responsible for her than you? So you decide the best thing to do is to stand in the middle of the street flagging down motorists, checking their licenses for violations or their vehicles for safety infractions. Or you take a totally different approach. You ignore the issue altogether. You never think about it or talk about it with your child. You busy yourself with other things instead. Ridiculous, isn't it? Yet people with eating disorders do parallel things with their feelings and life events. They use food as their mode of control and as a cover for feelings.

Controlling Emotions

The first and foremost method of control that people with eating disorders use on themselves is to deny their feelings. Dr. Richard Miller, the director of a drug treatment program near Sacramento, California, states, "Of all the drugs and compulsive behaviors that I have seen in the past twenty-five years, be it cocaine, heroin, alcohol, nicotine, gambling, sexual addiction, food addiction, all have one common thread. That is the covering up, or the masking, or the unwillingness on the part of the human being to confront and be with his or her human feelings." Though emotions and feelings -- like colors -- are neither good nor bad, many people nonetheless pass judgment on them. They say, "I shouldn't feel that way," or, "This feeling is too much for me to bear." So they put whatever they are feeling under wrap and out of view.

"I've never gotten angry in my life," said a compulsive eater. "Instead, my arms break out in a rash and I go to the food. Through food, I can create the feelings I want. I can be relaxed if I'm tense, excited if I'm bored, happy if I'm sad, or in control when I feel out of control." As one person put it, "I use fat to control living."

Another said, "The fear of not being perfect makes me purge and eat again. Yes, I'm a bulimic," she admitted. "The one area I'm not perfect is in control of my food."

"I have to eat," said another. "It's the only way I can get through Tony's leaving me." Can you feel the power and weight these words carry? They allow the person to think he or she is taking action on the situation when, in reality, all they are doing is promoting the addiction.

"It's the only way I can..." becomes a template for a legion of reasons that support the disease. For example, some say, "It's the only way I can get through my husband's lung cancer," or, "mother's anger at me," or "getting fired," or other "problems."

Exercise 35
Complete the statement below:
I have to eat (or purge, or be compulsive about food). It's the only way I can get through . . . . . .

True Control
Putting true control back in your life means you are going to be out of control at times. Taking charge involves letting go. It means you have to accept the reality that much of what happens to you and those around you is beyond your control.

But is this control, you argue?

Yes, because true control must always conform or address itself to reality. Control is as elusive as your breath. It's with you, but you can't hold onto it because it can't be held onto. If you hold your breath or breathe at an accelerated rate, problems arise. Why? The natural rhythm and flow of your breath is broken and it affects the proper functioning of the body as well as the mind. Your control, like your breath, must be accepted for the free spirit that it is.

Letting Go
What you do in letting go differs for everyone

and can vary according to the situation. Letting go does not mean giving up or letting others walk all over you. On the contrary, it means *doing everything humanly possible first and then letting go.* Listen to these three experiences of letting go:

Beth

"When the clutch on my car gave out, I immediately called my fiance for help," said Beth. "But after I related all that had happened, I suddenly realized that I myself could make the necessary phone calls to remedy the problem. So I told him I had it all under control. When the car mechanic informed me it would cost $500 for a new clutch, I said, 'I'll pay it.' But in my mind, I didn't know where I would get the money. Perhaps I could trim the holiday budget, or say goodbye to the department stores for a year. Somehow, I thought, I'd find a legitimate way to get that money through my own efforts.

"There would have been a time," she added, "when I would have instantly called my father and asked him for the money. Then I would have sobbed, and binged, and purged for days because he would have refused. I realized it was my responsibility. There were different ways I could handle it. And then, placing my trust in God, I let go."

Anne

Anne recounts the time her son entered second grade. "I could have requested a particular teacher," she said. "This is an option my school district offers. But I didn't take it. I wanted to let go and let the chips fall where they may. But as the term wore on, I noticed my son having problems. He didn't get along with his teacher. There were obvious personality conflicts.

"When I mentioned my dilemma at the next OA meeting, a number of the members, some of whom were school teachers, urged me to go back and do something. But I had let go, I explained, and now it seemed too late to do anything at all. I wanted to eat to ease the incessant frustration I felt. But they said no. I could go to my child and say, 'How would you feel if I asked your teacher to place you in another class?' Having obtained his approval, I could approach the teacher and ask if this were possible.

"At this point, I would have done all that is humanly possible, and then I had to abide by school policies and decisions. That is, I had to let go and let the results be. I did this, even though I was nervous and unsure about what would happen. My son is now in a different class and seems much more adjusted."

John

"I remember the time I was going to take the exam to become a certified alcoholism counselor. I studied and studied, constantly affirming to myself that I liked what I was doing and that I knew the material well. This was all I could possibly do to prepare for the test. Then I had to let go, and simply take the test and trust the outcome.

"But there was a time when the pressure was

so great that I would have skipped the test even though I'd studied as hard as I could. I couldn't face the possibility of failing. Instead, I'd prepare a three-course meal for two and eat it all myself. Now I say, 'I've done everything in my power to pass. Whether I pass or fail is something I can no longer control. I trust in God and in the process that whatever happens will be good for me'."

Exercise 36
What burden in life are you choosing to carry because you are afraid of what will happen if you choose to let go? Write that below.

"Good News -- Bad News -- Who Knows?"
This is an ancient tale that may shed some light about letting go.

Once there was an old farmer who had a large farm. One day one of his workers came running to him saying, "I have some bad news to tell you. Your horse ran away into the hills and is lost."

The farmer replied, "Good news, bad news, who knows?"

A week later the same hired hand ran again to the farmer, shouting, "Good news, sir! Your horse has returned with a herd of wild horses. Now you are richer than before."

The farmer replied, "Good news, bad news, who knows?"

Then as the farmer's son was trying to tame one of the horses, he fell. Running as fast as he could, the hired hand found the farmer and said, "I have some bad news for you. Your son broke his leg."

The farmer replied, "Good news, bad news, who knows?"

Some weeks later, the army marched into the village and signed up every able-bodied youth they found. The worker ran to the farmer and said, "Good news, sir! Because your son has a broken leg, they have not taken him."

And the farmer replied, "Good news, bad news, who knows?"

As this story clearly shows, often, things aren't what they seem. When deciding to change a situation or trying to make it better, it is wise to exercise control sparingly and appropriately.

A Healthy Sense Of Control

Of course, the trick is to know what you can change and what you can't. It involves knowing when to let go and when not. This wisdom is free and comes to everyone who wants it and is willing to wait for it.

Perhaps the words of the "serenity prayer" describe best how to attain a healthy sense of control. They are:

"God, grant me the serenity to accept
the things I cannot change,
The courage to change the things I can,
And the wisdom to know the difference."

Keeping these words uppermost in mind has helped many people realize a healthy sense of control and the peace that flows from it.

Exercise 37

a) What are some of the things in your life that you would like to change but cannot? List them below.

b) What are some of the things in your life that you would like to change and can? List them below.

c) For each item listed in "b", name one appropriate action you could take. Write that below.

Jot down below what you are feeling right now.

Chapter 8
Your Attitudes And You

*"I realize I like having the anger.
I don't want to give it up."*

What makes life so difficult for some and easier for others is not so much a difference in the set of events that happens to them, but a difference in how they react to these events -- in other words, their attitudes. The following story from the book *One Minute Wisdom* by Tony de Mello illustrates how a person's attitude affects his or her perception of reality. It is called "Happiness":

"I am in desperate need of help -- or I'll go crazy. We're living in a single room, my wife, my children, and my in-laws. So our nerves are on edge. We yell and scream at one another. The room is hell."

"Do you promise to do whatever I tell you?" said the master gravely.

"I swear I shall do anything."

"Very well. How many animals do you have?"

" A cow, a goat and six chickens."

"Take them all into the room with you. Then come back after a week."

The disciple was appalled. But he had promised to obey! So he took the animals in. A week later he came back, a pitiable figure, moaning, "I'm a nervous wreck. The dirt! The stench! The noise! We're all on the verge of madness!"

"Go back," said the master, "and put the animals out."

The man ran all the way home. He came back the following day, his eyes sparkling with joy. "How sweet life is! The animals are out. The home is a Paradise -- so quiet and clean and roomy!"

A Disease Of The Attitudes

Compulsive eaters operate out of a climate of negative attitudes. As a result, some people call compulsive eating a disease of the attitudes.

In talking about attitudes, one must see the fine line that distinguishes them from feelings. A feeling is a natural, spontaneous reaction to something that you perceive as happening or not happening to you. For instance, if your friend tells a lie about you, it's normal to experience hurt and anger at that person. But after you've communicated your feeling of hurt and anger to your friend, you've allowed those feelings to dissipate because they've been expressed appropriately.

An attitude, on the other hand, is a pattern of thought and behavior that develops over the course of time as a result of or as a reaction to these feelings. If, in the example above, you keep re-feeling the hurt and anger over and over instead of communicating it with your friend, you have invited your feelings to re-fuel in you. Before you know it, an attitude of resentment or hostility develops in you. That becomes your emotional style or stance that defines everything else you feel, think and do. It's the atmospheric pressure in which you move and breathe. It even affects your body posture as the muscles in your face, neck, torso and limbs position themselves to reflect the degree of tension, stress or relaxation present inside you. Feelings come unbidden. Attitudes require your permission to grow and reside in you. While feelings are never good nor bad but simply there to be recognized, experienced and expressed appropriately, attitudes can be positive or negative. Positive attitudes foster health and wholeness both in mind and body. Negative attitudes promote disease, and a dis-ease of body and mind. When compulsive eaters act out of their disease, they operate under a climate of negative attitudes.

Exercise 38
Think of a situation where you re-fueled a feeling you had and it developed into a negative attitude? How did it affect your behavior? Write that below.

An Attitude Of Denial
Compulsive eaters are immersed in denial. They deny how they look, act, think and feel. At times they even deny who they are.

"I hated my body my whole life. Growing up, I saw myself enlarge in the wrong places at the wrong times," said a bulimic mother of three. "It's strange, I never saw myself as short though I'm under five feet tall," she added, "but I always saw myself as fat."

"I never look in a mirror. I still see myself as I was fourteen years ago, before I put on all this weight," said one man.

"I wear a bra that's a size smaller than I need. I always see myself as small. It's how I was before," said one woman.

"I forget about my body. I concern myself more with my hair and my nails," said another.

"The 'spinster school-marm look' is for me. I wear only loose fitting jumpers until they get too tight. The reality that I am expanding under these clothes is something I don't dwell on," added a third.

"Recently, I didn't recognize my face in a photo. 'Who is that?' I asked. I couldn't believe it was me!" said one man.

Exercise 39
What reality or aspects of your life are you not facing through an attitude of denial? Write them below.

An Attitude Of Anger And Resentment

Anger usually covers a hurt of some kind. "My father always said, 'You don't love God if you allow yourself to get this big.' So I gained 360 pounds just to show him," said one woman.

Resentment is anger that has not been given free and appropriate expression. Recall the study on addicted personalities which revealed that the inability to express feelings, along with the physical aspect of addiction, is more a cause than an effect of the addiction. What researchers conclude is that somehow there's a malfunctioning in the emotional mechanism of the addicted person. Compulsive eaters have to be taught how to let go and express their feelings appropriately.

Resentment is anger buried alive. "I can picture anger lowered in a coffin and I just keep piling the dirt on," said one man.

What are some of the things that make compulsive eaters angry and resentful? It could be anything and everything. It could stem from childhood as one compulsive eater shared. "I'm really angry at my mother dying when I was four," he said. "I don't think I would necessarily have gotten addicted to food that early. I know my addiction has a physical dependence, but I think I could have been nurtured in other ways. I would have had two parents to bounce things off. Perhaps my father would not have been an alcoholic if my mother had lived."

Others might be angry at a more recent situation. "I'm angry because I have to go out to work when I don't want to," said one woman.

"I don't like the way my life has turned out," said another.

Exercise 40
What angry feelings are you keeping buried inside you? What might happen if you let them out by expressing them? Write that below.

Other Attitudes
There are countless other attitudes that compulsive eaters display. One is *isolation*. "I think it doesn't matter when no one sees you," said one woman. She described how she cuts a cake horizontally from the bottom in order to eat some without anyone else knowing a piece was cut. The cake is now lower but still seemingly intact.

"I eat in a room where no one can watch me eat," said another.

"I've eaten off other people's plates when they're not looking," said a third.

Another attitude is that of *blaming other things or other people.* "I have my period," said one woman.

"I wear a suit that's too small so that I can put the blame on other's perception of me," said one man. "I tell myself if they can't handle it, it's their problem -- not mine."

A third attitude is *ingratitude.* Rather than focusing on life's blessings, the focus is more on the hardships or what's missing. "I'm not grateful. I'm angry!" said a compulsive eater emphatically.

Changing Your Attitudes

Can you move from one attitude to another, from one way of acting to another? This is how Karen did it:

"When I learned that my youngest sister who was getting married had asked my other two sisters to be in her wedding party, but not me, I was hurt," she began. "Thoughts of not showing up for the wedding, anger and resentment at the way I'd been treated, consumed me.

"I could see the hurt come from far away. I recognized it instantly. It was like a giant block of cement, a cube about ten feet high, slowly easing in my direction as if I were a magnet pulling it towards me. It was the same hurt I'd received other times when I felt left out, especially by my family. I knew I didn't want it. It was too much to bear. But I couldn't stop it from approaching.

"Suddenly in my mind, I stepped back out of its way for a moment. I thought, I can embrace this hurt because I know how much I'd love to be in the wedding party. Why am I not in it? I'm always excluded. But if I take this block, it'll energize my hurt and I'll continue to hurt. No, I thought. I don't want to hurt like this!

"Then I noticed that the giant block had stopped moving. It seemed to be waiting for my cue before it could go on. I became aware of the tremendous power I had.

"I can have two attitudes on this. I can choose to be hurt and this block will get nearer and nearer and it will eat me up. Or I can say to myself, 'How nice it would have been if my sister had asked me. But, she didn't.' I pondered,' Should I let that stop me from having a good time at the wedding?' 'No,' I decided. I accept the situation as it is. I asked myself, 'What's the best thing I can make of this for me?' I chose to be grateful to go to the wedding instead of resentful that I hadn't been asked to be in the wedding party.

"To my surprise, the block of cement vanished. As the wedding neared, I kept waiting and watching just in case the cement block returned. I felt that in touch with my feelings. But the cement block never came back. I guess the hurt knew it wasn't welcome any longer."

Exercise 41
Think of a time when your behavior changed because you changed your attitude? Describe that below.

Jot down what you are feeling right now.

Chapter 9
The Power To Choose

"I didn't know I had a choice."

"Life is meant to be more than living on potato chips," said one woman at the end of a compulsive eaters retreat. "When is it going to change? I'm 46, I feel like 56, and look like 66. I'm so humiliated. I'm intelligent and a college graduate, but I continue to eat compulsively. I hate myself for it, and yet I can't stop," she cried.

"Will I ever recover from this disease?" asked one man.

Another participant blurted out, "What am I going to do now? If I had the flu, I'd go to the doctor. Will I go to OA? I don't know."

The power to choose rests with each individual, yet the irony is that many compulsive eaters feel powerless in the face of their own potency. They are not aware that the decision to stay in their disease or to get out of it lies directly in their own hands. Consciously or unconsciously, they often choose not to exercise that power. They choose to give it away, instead, in various ways.

Fears And Excuses

Compulsive eaters let many fears and excuses absorb the power and responsibility for their choices.

69

"I can't give up food. I'm afraid I won't know what to do with my feelings," said one woman.

Others may be unwilling to do the work. "Lying is my natural state. Honesty takes effort," said one man.

"I'm tired of therapy because all they do is re-hash what's in the past and I don't want to do that," said another.

Some are not prepared to make commitments. "I don't want to say I'm going to do something and then not do it," said one woman.

"I haven't been ready to deal with my anger. I've been stuffing it instead," said a man.

Others may not know what to do, where to go or who to ask for proper help. "I've spent my whole life dieting -- since I was eighteen. I've tried everything, but nothing works," said one woman.

Exercise 42
What excuses are you using to give your power and responsibility away? List them below.

The Right Timing
When people present excuses, it usually means they're unwilling to deal with their disease. The excuse is their way of relieving themselves of all responsibility and action at that moment.

"If not now, when?" said one compulsive

eater.

Everyone's threshold for pain is different. Each person has his or her own time clock for action. When that time comes, you will know it. Here's a story that helps to illustrate this.

Moment of Decision

There was a man who, in order to get to where he wanted to go, found himself in front of a tunnel. When he entered it, he discovered it was a holding ground for a cesspool. At first, he was appalled and thought of turning back to look for a different route. But, since he wasn't sure of another way, he pressed on. If some of the filth went on his shoes, he rationalized, he could always wipe it off walking or scrape it along the wall. But soon it was all around him and getting quite deep. When it started to rise up the legs of his pants, he became a little concerned.

"Not to worry," he said. "I'll change my clothes when I arrive and send these to be cleaned." But as he continued, the filth rose higher and higher and finally reached his shirt, covering his hands.

"At least it's not on my face." He exhaled a sigh of relief. No sooner did he say this than he felt it slowly touching the back of his neck.

"At least, I'm able to breathe," he said reassured. Then as the filth trickled into his mouth, he decided he could bear it no longer. Just then he had an idea. If he kept his mouth closed, he could hold on as long as his nose remained free. But each step forward sank him deeper down. Finally, he decided he'd had enough. There had to be a better way to where he was going. He turned around and went back to look for it.

At what point would you have turned back if you had been the man in the story?

Exactly when the moment of decision is for someone to recover from his or her addiction, no one can say but that person. "I had to hit physical, spiritual, and emotional bottom before I could begin recovery," said a bulimic.

"I guess I've wasted enough time. I'm going to do something about my disease now," said one compulsive eater.

"I'm going to go to a meeting. I'm going to get a sponsor. I won't die from this pain," said another.

"I'm taking that first step. I'm going to an OA meeting today," said a third.

Exercise 43
What are you willing to do about your disease? Describe below.

Being Responsible For Yourself
For compulsive eaters, making choices affects several areas. The first area is to be responsible for oneself. One woman recently out of rehab asked her husband, "Are you willing to do all you have to do for me to maintain my abstinence?" In posing this

question, the woman, instead of being responsible for herself, was giving away to her husband her own power and responsibility to stay abstinent. Thus, whenever her husband chose not to cooperate, it would give her the legitimate excuse she sought to binge.

"I have to do it. No one else can do it for me," a compulsive eater wisely reflected. When you don't choose for yourself but let others decide for you, you are a victim. To recover from anything, you have to make choices all along.

People who choose to be responsible for themselves accept and express appropriately all their feelings, both positive and negative. They make an effort to understand their feelings and accept the consequences of sharing them. At the same time, they are aware that expressing their feelings is not an end to their pain but a beginning to how to deal with it.

People responsible for themselves let their standards of conduct reflect who they really are, what they really think, and not what others expect from them. They do not allow fears and inhibitions to control their life, but seek ways to overcome them instead. They look for the good in themselves and others as well. They think of themselves in positive terms and make allowances for occasional failures. "I won't be 'guilted' into action or non-action so as not to disappoint someone's expectations of me," said one retreatant.

Self-responsible people become increasingly assertive without being aggressive. They expect to be respected and taken seriously because they represent themselves without violating others. They refuse to rescue others and refuse to let others rescue them. As persons who are responsible for their own choices, they direct their own lives as much as possible without seeking control over others or becoming subservient to them.

Relationship And Time Choices

The second and third areas of choice-making involve relationship and time choices. Making relationship choices means seeking out people with whom you can be fully honest. This is crucial because being dishonest triggers compulsive eaters back into their disease. Also a true friend will make no demands. He or she will not run guilt trips on you for something you should or shouldn't have done. In relationships, you'll find you'll need to set up personal boundaries that are fair to you and others.

In addition, you'll need to make choices about time. One compulsive eater said, "There's never enough for me -- never enough food, never enough in a relationship, never enough time." You'll need to adjust how much time you have to give. You need to let go of some things that demand your time in preference for others more important to recovery.

Surrendering Through The 12-Steps

"I'm a compulsive eater. I can't do it alone," said one woman.

"I'm a compulsive eater. I want to find out why," said another.

"I'm a compulsive eater. I need to start some sort of program," said a third.

Surrendering to God through the 12 Steps is the fourth area of choice-making. The Twelve Step Program of AA that works so well for alcoholics in recovery works equally well for compulsive eaters in recovery. The only difference is that wherever the words "alcohol" and "alcoholic" appear, they are changed to "food" and "compulsive overeater."

Here are the steps as adapted for Overeaters Anonymous.

Twelve Steps -- Overeaters Anonymous

1. We admitted we were powerless over food, that our lives had become unmanageable.

2. Came to believe that a Power greater than ourselves could restore us to sanity.

3. Made a decision to turn our will and our lives over to the care of God *as we understood Him.*

4. Made a searching and fearless moral inventory of ourselves.

5. Admitted to God, to ourselves and to another human being the exact nature of our wrongs.

6. Were entirely ready to have God remove all these defects of character.

7. Humbly asked Him to remove our shortcomings.

8. Made a list of all persons we had harmed, and became willing to make amends to them all.

9. Made direct amends to such people wherever possible, except when to do so would

injure them or others.

10. Continued to take personal inventory and when we were wrong, promptly admitted it.

11. Sought through prayer and meditation to improve our conscious contact with God *as we understood Him,* praying only for knowledge of His will for us and the power to carry that out.

12. Having had a spiritual awakening as the result of these steps, we tried to carry this message to compulsive overeaters and to practice these principles in all our affairs.

"I finally put cotton in my mouth and took it out of my ears," said Paul as he described his decision to start the program.

Another said, "My sponsor took me through the steps."

A third remembered, "My sponsor kept asking me, 'What are you willing to do for your recovery?' I hated the question. It's painful to recover. Yet holding on to the disease was more painful."

"I was asked, 'Are you the kind of person you want to come home to?'" said Vivian. "I knew the answer to that question immediately."

The steps build one upon the other and are worked on one at a time, in the order given, and on a daily basis. "I call myself a recovering bulimic," said one woman. "I work my recovery one day at a time."

"For me recovery started on a physical level. I worked the program very mechanically at first. Now, it's a part of my life," said another.

OA (Overeaters Anonymous) Fellowship

The OA fellowship is the support group for those following the 12-Steps. It is not a "diet and calories" club, but rather a group of people who meet together to talk and listen to other compulsive overeaters. Most people who attend make an important discovery at their very first meeting. They realize they are in the clutches of a dangerous illness and that willpower, emotional health and self-confidence are no defense against it.

Members read OA and AA literature with an open mind and are willing to rely on a power greater than themselves for direction in their lives. They take the twelve steps and follow them faithfully to the best of their ability in order to recover from their disease.

The fellowship welcomes anyone and everyone who wants to stop eating compulsively. There are no dues or fees. Each group is self-supporting through members' own contributions, neither soliciting nor accepting outside donations. Also OA is not affiliated with any public or private organization, political movement, ideology or religious doctrine. It takes no position on outside issues.

How did such a fellowship come to be? It evolved through the efforts of a woman who was married to a gambler. One day this woman attended a Gamblers Anonymous meeting. As she listened to the 12 Steps being explained and shared there, she admitted that she had a problem with food and this method of recovery could also work for her.

She wrote down the 12 Steps and later began

to meet with another person. In the process, she did a lot of paraphrasing and shifting of words to come up with 12 Steps for OA. She personally didn't want any mention of God, so she decided to take those words out. But the program didn't work this way. The woman found she had to go back to the original AA steps and follow them exactly as they were, changing only the words alcohol and alcoholic to food and compulsive overeater.

In addition to the 12-Steps, the OA fellowship also follows the twelve traditions of AA. Here are the twelve traditions as adapted for OA:

Twelve Traditions of OA

1. Our common welfare should come first; personal recovery depends upon OA unity.

2. For our group purposes there is but one ultimate authority -- a loving God as He may express Himself in our group conscience. Our leaders are but trusted servants; they do not govern.

3. The only requirement for OA membership is a desire to stop eating compulsively.

4. Each group should be autonomous except in matters affecting other groups or OA as a whole.

5. Each group has but one primary purpose -- to carry its message to the compulsive overeater who still suffers.

6. An OA group ought never endorse, finance or lend the OA name to any related facility or outside enterprise, lest problems of money, property and prestige divert us from our primary purpose.

7. Every OA group ought to be fully self-supporting, declining outside contributions.

8. Overeaters Anonymous should remain forever non-professional, but our service centers may employ special workers.

9. OA, as such, ought never to be organized; but we may create service boards or committees directly responsible to those they serve.

10. Overeaters Anonymous has no opinion on outside issues; hence the OA name ought never be drawn into public controversy.

11. Our public relations policy is based on attraction rather than promotion; we need always maintain personal anonymity at the level of press, radio, films, television, and other public media of communication.

12. Anonymity is the spiritual foundation of all these traditions, ever reminding us to place principles before personalities.

Initially, almost everyone exhibits a resistance to the OA fellowship.

"When my therapist said to go to OA, I told him to go to hell," said one compulsive eater.

"I had a fear of joining OA and giving my control to someone else," said another.

But after a period of time and deliberation, the fellowship is seen in a different light. "I'm willing to do what it takes not to take that first bite," said one man.

"I'm willing to start taking some risks in my life," said another.

Both the 12 Steps and the OA fellowship are needed to sustain an on-going recovery. A program of recovery that uses one without the other limps. "After going to OA, I don't think diet anymore. I have come away with much more," said a compulsive eater.

Owning Your Power

In the book, *Return To The Garden*, author Shakti Gawain said, "...if you have repressed your power, you will have anger building up inside of you." You have to own your power instead of letting it own you.

Who is your power arsenal? It's you! Many compulsive eaters are not aware of this. *You* have the power to choose. No longer do you have to let the food define you. You can choose positive attitudes that lead to healthy behavior. There can be problems in your life, but you can choose not to be victimized by them. You can have feelings of anger, resentment and helplessness, but you can choose not to be enslaved by them.

Exercise 44
Are you ready to own your power? What choice do you need to make today for your own recovery? Write that below:

Jot down what you are feeling right now.

Chapter 10
The Right To Set Boundaries

"When I'm into food, anyone can invade my boundaries."

Many changes happen to people in recovery during the recovery process, both outside and within. For example, their bodies will be healthier, more attractive and energetic. Their confidence level and positive self-image will improve. This is wonderful for the recovering person but it can cause problems for others. Some people will have difficulty reacting to these changes. Therefore, it begins to be more than chance or choice for the first bite. It begins to be chance or choice for actions and recovery methods involving yourself. You will come to points where it seems almost easier to back down about certain things that will be asked of you that will ultimately affect your food use. Now it becomes no longer decisions about food. It's decisions about communication, relationships and life as well.

Dealing With The Many Changes
At this point, you will need to set some boundaries in order to deal successfully with others' reactions to the fact that you are changing. You'll also need to communicate what these changes are to others so that they know where you're coming from. Remember, they're expecting the old you. You'll have to tell them of the new you. You'll need

to share with them the changes you are undergoing. You'll want to ask them if they accept these changes. Will you have to negotiate them? Will you have to set limits for the non-negotiable ones? In her book, *Fat Is A Family Affair*, Judy Hollis states, "I had to renegotiate every relationship in my life."

These are things that do not happen overnight. They take time. If you think it's scary for you, think how scary it is for others. In their interaction with a changing you, their sense of security and relationship with you is threatened.

Living With Boundaries

Some people say they can't live with boundaries, but boundaries are all around. You need not fear them. You live with them everyday. The whole world is made up of boundaries.

A boundary is something that indicates a limit, specifically a bounding point or separating line between people or things. Here are a few examples of world or outside boundaries: A 30 mph sign on a residential street limits how fast you can drive on it; you can't put 13 ounces into a 12 ounce diet soda can; national, state, city or county borders define under whose laws residents and visitors must operate.

There are also personal boundaries. Visually, they can be seen as a space bubble that surrounds a person. This is the edge between one person and another, where the first person stops and the other begins. Some examples of personal boundaries are: "No, you may not borrow my car," or "I only have fifteen minutes before my appointment, but I'd be glad to talk with you for that length of time," or "I'm surprised you asked me that. I'd rather not say." Others might be, "I will not allow myself to be abused," or "I will not eat flour, or sugar (or other addictive food)."

Exercise 45
Think of a few personal boundaries that you are currently working at trying to establish, or struggling with in your life. Write them below.

How Boundaries Are Formed
How do boundaries come to be? How are they developed? Where are they developed? It all happens in that great system called family of origin.

All families of origin, both healthy and dysfunctional, will model two things: how to nurture oneself and how to be in intimate relationships with others. And this is what personal boundaries are all about.

Boundaries are set from within because that's where they come from. You already know what some of them are for you. "I can't talk to anyone until after I've had my first cup of coffee," said one woman.

"Once I make a commitment, I don't break it," said one man.

There are some boundary issues you may not even be aware of until people bring them to your attention.

"Once, at an OA meeting, I shared how someone had asked me for a personal item. I would have felt violated if I'd given it to that person, so I lied and said I couldn't find it," explained one man. "One of the people present said, 'You can't say no to that person.' I couldn't believe it! He was right!"

Sometimes events make you aware of personal boundaries you have or need to set. "I realize I made a mistake with a person at work this week," said one woman. "I didn't set a time limit for our meetings. Because she's open-ended with time and I'm on a rather tight schedule, I'm sometimes left hanging as to when our sessions will end. This paralyzes me; I can't make plans for after the meeting until the meeting actually ends. And I hate it."

Exercise 46
a) State a personal boundary that comes from your family of origin. b) Recall an event or person who made you aware that you needed to set a personal boundary. Write that below.

Setting And Maintaining Boundaries
Boundaries have to do with self-respect and self-esteem. When these two issues get violated, it's

a clue that a boundary needs to be set. How do you know what boundary to set? A good gauge is to reflect on the situation that violated something inside you and see what it tells you.

"Every time I called my mother on the phone, she put a lot of pressure on me to see her instantly," said Vivian. "If I went over there, I was resentful. If I didn't, I felt guilty. I hate to be pressured. Then I realized the pattern that was happening here every time. So I decided that I would call my mother only at a time I was free to see her. Guess what? I'm no longer resentful when I visit."

"I have to establish boundaries with the enablers in my life. I will not hand over the responsibility for my disease or my person to them," said one woman.

Sometimes, conferring with people who know you and whom you trust is the verification you need to go ahead and set a certain boundary.

"Many times I check with my sponsor. 'Is this a good boundary?' I ask. 'Can I use it with so and so?'" said Paul. This also gives the boundary a high success rate of being maintained.

Evaluating existing boundaries from time to time is also a good idea. Are they producing the results you need? Are they failing? Are they too strong? Are they not strong enough?

How do you continue to set and maintain appropriate boundaries? You work on them constantly by reflecting, evaluating, changing and adapting them as necessary. If any boundary you are now using doesn't work, you might want to renegotiate it with others. There might be another way you could get what you need that others can accept.

Exercise 47
Set a boundary that you need right now. Write it below.

Communicating Boundaries

Always remember to communicate the boundary or boundary change. A boundary that is not communicated is like no boundary at all.

Many times, a compulsive eater will try to communicate boundaries through food, fat, silence or slamming of doors. These are all indirect and inappropriate approaches. When people come to recovery, they are taught to communicate boundaries with open, direct and congruent speech.

Be clear and authentic. Don't communicate a boundary that you really don't mean, aren't going to keep, or can't enforce. For example, if you say "No, I do not accept phone calls after 10 p.m.," but then go ahead and answer the phone when it rings after 10, perhaps you really didn't mean that boundary. If you meant it, you would find ways to enforce it. How? You could unplug your phone, or not answer it, or you'd have others answer it and say you're not available. Another example involves your teenage son's wish to borrow your car. You say no. But he keeps asking and eventually you break down and say yes. You didn't mean this boundary strong enough. There was something in you that said you weren't sure, that you really didn't mean the no and your son picked it up.

When you change a boundary, you have to communicate that change also. For example, "I've been letting you use the phone in my office for quick calls while I'm there. I would like to ask now that you no longer use the phone while I'm there. Can you accept that?"

Exercise 48
State a boundary you have set and mean to enforce. How would you communicate it and to whom? Write that below.

State a set boundary you need to change. How would you communicate this? Write that below.

Non-Negotiable Boundaries

Some boundaries are non-negotiable. What do you do here? The very same thing. You communicate directly what the boundary is and ask if the other person accepts it. Here is how Carl and Marsha handled a non-negotiable boundary that Carl had.

"I'm a recovering alcoholic," Carl said. "When I first asked Marsha for a date, she didn't know that. So I told her that I didn't do bars or clubs. I also told her that if she wanted to go to those places, I couldn't date her. I gave her a choice to accept or refuse my non-negotiable boundary. She told me she wanted to date me and was willing not to do bars or clubs."

Other non-negotiable boundaries might be smoking, dining in all-you-can-eat restaurants, skipping meals.

Exercise 49
What are some of your non-negotiable boundaries? How do you communicate them to others? Write that below.

When Others Invade Your Boundaries, Explore Your Options

Most people are respectful of boundaries especially if they have been clearly and courteously communicated. But just as there are people who break laws, there are people who will invade your boundaries no matter how conscientious you are in setting and maintaining them.

When someone invades your boundaries what recourse do you have? You don't have to feel trapped or stuck. There are choice or response options to questions and actions that invade your boundaries. Exploring what these options might be for you and practicing them privately is a twin lesson in diplomacy and freedom.

"At a business meeting someone once asked me if I minded telling how much my new suit cost," said Vivian. "I was appalled at her intrusion and felt put on the spot. Remembering that I wasn't compelled to answer the question in only one way, I said, 'I'd rather not say.' Since then, I've learned other options to use with such questions, such as 'I choose not to answer that question', or, to say very directly, 'Yes, I do mind.'"

"I used to give a nervous laugh when people asked me personal questions I would rather not answer," said one man. "But since I became aware that I had options in my responses at such times, I don't lose my composure as much and I keep my privacy intact," he added.

"I won't accept being screamed at. When someone, for example, my son or daughter, screams at me I now leave the room. It's much better than screaming back in retaliation like I used to," said a mother of teenagers.

"Sometimes I look back and realize how badly I handled a boundary invasion. Rather than berate myself, I imagine how else I could have handled it. I practice these other options in front of a mirror so that next time I'm better equipped," said Paul.

Exercise 50
State a personal boundary that others have invaded. Explore and imagine different ways of handling the situation. Write what they are at the top of the next page. If the response is verbal, practice that in front of a mirror until it sounds comfortable. If the

response is an action, practice that several times until it feels comfortable.

Questions To Raise Related To Boundaries
   * What is the line between self-caring and selfishness?
   * Do I have the right to determine what is acceptable behavior to me and what is non-acceptable?
   * Do I have the right to set boundaries toward those I love?
   * Do I have the right to set boundaries toward those for whom I'm responsible?
   * Do I have the right to set boundaries towards others in the 12 Step program?
   * What are my non-negotiable boundaries?
   * What are my negotiable boundaries?
   * Can I set different boundaries with different people?
   * How do I react when another invades my boundaries?
   * How do I act or react to another's boundaries?

Boundary Statements Your Heart
Will Recognize
   * There's no me.

* I'm giving out.
* A bankruptcy's happening.
* I can't talk to you today. I'm getting space for myself.
* I could separate from the person. If I were into alcohol, food, or some other substance, I couldn't separate myself.
* If you try to set another's boundaries for them which is their responsibility, such as telling them not to drink, that's control.
* Only I can set my own boundaries. No one else can or should set them for me.
* I'm aware of other people's boundaries and I won't encroach upon them, but I have difficulty claiming my own so that other people don't encroach on mine.
* Some boundaries I don't even know I have until they're threatened or invaded.
* I feel anger when some people get through my boundaries.
* There will be times I will choose to allow my boundary to be invaded and it will be okay because the choice is mine.
* If I state a boundary but don't mean it, others know and don't respect it.
* There's no sense making boundaries I won't be able to keep.
* Boundaries depend on the knowledge of who I am and who I'm not and who you are and who you're not.

Jot down what you are feeling right now.

Chapter 11
Forgiving Yourself And Others

"Until I forgave, I couldn't go on with life!"

One of the hardest areas to deal with in recovery is that of forgiveness. How do you forgive all the harm that's done to you and others because of your food addiction? Yet the ability to forgive is most significant. It brings about unimagined healing, freedom and peace.

In an article on forgiveness, Doris Donnelly recounts the story of Kay, divorced and mother of three children. Kay admitted that the last thing on her mind when she and her husband went their separate ways was to forgive him. Three years later, she recalled:

"When I finally forgave, I no longer needed my family, friends and co-workers to take sides with me against David. I no longer perpetuated a despairing cycle of non-forgiveness in relationships. I was able to establish friendships without dragging my feelings for David with me.

"It was probably the most exciting day of my life when I noticed that I was no longer directed by my pain. When I broke the cycle of non-forgiving, I became a self-determining person who was no longer towed around reacting to someone else's behavior."

Ending Destructive Behavior

To forgive is to cease to blame or to cease to feel resentment against someone. Continual blaming of another shows you haven't let go. You're still holding on to obsessed hatred. It plays on you like a broken record and causes havoc to your mental, emotional, and physical state.

"I always blamed my Mom for everything that happened to me," said Bob. "As long as I blamed her, I was bitter, angry and into the food. I couldn't get on with my life because I tried to punish her with my behavior. Instead, I found I was punishing myself more than her, and many times, instead of her. Once I stopped blaming and started to take responsibility for my own actions, the resentment began to leave me and I was able to forgive her."

Exercise 51
Recall a time when you forgave someone. Describe how you felt before you forgave and then how you felt afterwards.

Accepting The Past

Forgiveness is accepting the past, but this doesn't mean carrying it. Many walk through life holding on to suitcases of past hurts, experiences, angers which become the unfinished emotional business in their lives. They never take the time to open up these suitcases and examine the contents. What are they carrying? Can they sort it out so that they can keep what's usable and throw out what's not? Compulsive eaters don't do that. They insist on carrying the excess emotional baggage of their lives, letting it weigh and wear them down.

Exercise 52
What excess emotional baggage are you walking around with? Describe that below.

Be Gentle With Yourself
"But there are things in my life that not only do I *not* want to forgive, but I also have trouble accepting," said a compulsive eater. "I've had to look at my life and distinguish which things I could accept and forgive and which I could not," said another.

"I've come to accept the fact that there are certain things I can't forgive!" said a third.

Exercise 53
Make two columns. Put what you can forgive on one side, what you can't forgive, on the other.

Accepting The Future

Forgiveness is accepting the future. This does not mean being resigned to whatever happens. On the contrary, it means doing all you possibly can in the present to promote a happy and healthy future. Once this is done, however, the future, like the past, must be let go. You must stop fretting about it. Otherwise it, too, can become excess emotional baggage.

"Most of us miss our own lives. Most of us spend our time preparing for a moment that never comes, while the years slip by, unnoticed, unused," states Geneen Roth in her book *Breaking Free*. "We often forget that our lives are made up of moments and of feelings about moments," she continues. "As compulsive eaters, we spend our lives forsaking all the moments of satisfaction for a future moment when we will be thin and the deprivation will have paid off. And if and when that moment does come, we are so worried about gaining weight that we focus our attention once more on the future and do not take pleasure in the present."

Exercise 54
What future events can you accept? What future events can you not accept? Make two columns below:

Living In the Present

The present moment is all there is. You accept the past for what it has been and the future for what it may be so that the present can be lived. Living in the present is to be responsible for yourself today. Don't dwell on what you or someone else could have done or should have done in a past situation. That moment is gone. Ask yourself, what can you do now? Your responsibility includes not bringing up the past as an excuse or reason to blame. Accepting the past for what it is, and, then, letting it go is the kind of "clean living" that helps to keep unnecessary residue away.

Life offers many opportunities to forgive, but one must be awake to them. In one compulsive eaters retreat, the film "Pardon and Peace" was shown as part of the forgiveness presentation. Two participants happened to be mother and daughter.

As soon as the film was over, the daughter began to share about her teenage years and how her behavior as a teen had hurt her mother. At that moment, she was given permission to take any appropriate action to which she felt drawn. The daughter got up, went over to her mother, knelt down in front of her and asked for her forgiveness.

The daughter lived the moment by taking responsibility for it. The film enabled her to stop blaming herself and freed her to forgive herself. Being thus freed, she could recognize and act on an opportunity to be forgiven.

Whom Do You Forgive?

Everyone and everything, including yourself. That means your parents, your friends, your relatives, your enemies, even your food. It sounds like a tall order and it is. But it's not done all at once but over a period of time. It takes into account the growth and readiness of the person forgiving and the opportunities that present themselves or that can be created for forgiveness to take place.

Some people say you have to forgive yourself first before you can forgive others. Others say you have to forgive other people before you can forgive yourself. Others, still, say it happens simultaneously. The process is different for each person.

"There are times in my life I find I have to forgive others," said one compulsive eater.

"There are days I have to forgive myself," said another.

Exercise 55
Is there anyone you feel you have to forgive today? Write their names below. (Remember, you may use code names or initials.) Do you have to forgive yourself today? If so, include your name among the list.

It's Never Too Late
"After I made a compulsive eaters retreat," said one woman, "I realized I hadn't forgiven my father for something that happened a long time ago. I hadn't seen nor spoken to him in over two years. Since he lived in another state, it had not been hard for me to maintain this separation. But then his birthday came up and a party was planned. I decided to fly down to see him. It was just the opportunity I needed to ask his forgiveness. We had a wonderful reconciliation. Within a few days of having flown back home, I received the news that he had died. I was so glad I had acted when I did. If I hadn't, just think what I would be living with now."

But then from another compulsive eater comes this account: "My mother died long before I realized I needed her forgiveness. Growing up, I expected so much from her and when I repeatedly didn't get it, I shut down with her. I didn't want her to see my feelings and in so doing, I shut down with myself as well. I stopped feeling so she couldn't get a sense of who I was any longer. Years later, in my forties, when I was the age she was when I lived at home, I began to look at things from her perspective. I realized how difficult it must have been for her -- a widow raising four children during wartime. So I went to her grave and asked for her forgiveness there."

The Prayer Of St. Francis

One woman shared how her relationship with her mother was eating her alive. All her life, she desperately sought her mother's love and approval but never felt successful in getting it. She idolized her mother. As a result, she grew up both loving and hating her mother. Filled with shame and remorse, she hated herself for feeling this way.

One day, someone suggested that she let go of all expectations from her mother, and simply recite one or more lines from the Prayer of St. Francis several times on a daily basis. After six months, the woman found that her hate for her mother was gone. She was now able to see her mother in a new light and accept the mother's shortcomings as well as her own. With this, she was free to love her mother without needing her mother to love her back, (though she would gladly accept it if it happened).

Meditating over the Prayer of St. Francis has been for many a powerful tool that brought them peace, love, and forgiveness. Here is the prayer as it appears in the book *Twelve Steps and Twelve Traditions* of AA:

Prayer of St. Francis
Lord, make me a channel of your peace
-- that where there is hatred, I may bring love
-- that where there is wrong, I may bring the
     spirit of forgiveness
-- that where there is discord, I may bring
     harmony
-- that where there is error, I may bring truth
-- that where there is doubt, I may bring faith
-- that where there is despair, I may bring
     hope
-- that where there are shadows, I may
     bring light
-- that where there is sadness, I may bring
     joy.

Lord, grant that I may seek rather to
     comfort than to be comforted
-- to understand, than to be understood
-- to love, than to be loved.
For it is by self-forgetting that one finds.
It is by forgiving that one is forgiven.
It is by dying that one awakens
     to Eternal Life.
Amen.

Exercise 56

Choose one line (the one that draws you) from the Prayer of St. Francis and, applying it to yourself, recite it several times for as long as you wish. Now choose the same line or another and recite it several times, applying it to a person you haven't forgiven.

The Fruits Of Forgiveness

Perhaps the fruits of forgiveness are best expressed by quoting the Promises from the Big Book of AA:

Promises

"We are going to know a new freedom and a new happiness. We will not regret the past nor wish to shut the door on it. We will comprehend the word serenity and we will know peace. No matter how far down the scale we have gone, we will see how our experience can benefit others. That feeling of uselessness and self-pity will disappear. We will lose interest in selfish things and gain interest in our fellows.

"Self-seeking will slip away. Our whole attitude and outlook upon life will change. Fear of people and of economic insecurity will leave us. We will intuitively know how to handle situations which used to baffle us. We will suddenly realize that God is doing for us what we could not do for ourselves.

"Are these extravagant promises? We think not. They are being fulfilled among us -- sometimes quickly, sometimes slowly. They will always materialize if we work for them."

Exercise 57
Fill in the blanks

My "Child"
I forgive you_____
I accept your forgiveness_____
Symbol of forgiving myself in
a relationship from childhood

My "Adult"
I forgive you _____
I accept your forgiveness_____
Symbol of forgiving myself in
an adult relationship.

My "Self"
I forgive you_____
I accept your forgiveness_____
Symbol of forgiving myself
right now.

Jot down what you are feeling right now.

Chapter 12
God

"I hung up on my sponsor when she talked about God."

"I hated hearing people talk about God," said one compulsive eater. "I had no connection. I felt doomed because for me there is no spiritual power."

"I feel totally abandoned by God. We have nothing in common," said another.

Images of God
Whether someone believes in God or not, he or she has an image of God. But not all people are aware of what that image is or that they operate out of it. See what the following exercise reveals to you. There are four parts to the exercise.

Exercise 58

Part 1:
Match the people in column "B" with the feeling words in column "A". You may use more than one word from column "A" to describe a person.

That First Bite

-A-	-B-
a. compulsive	1. Jean Nidetch
b. fat	2. Leo Buscaglia
c. isolated	3. Shirley MacLaine
d. peaceful	4. Mama Cass
e. powerful	5. Jesse Jackson
f. thin	6. Gloria Steinem
g. powerless	7. James Coco
h. domineering	8. Karen Carpenter
i. loving	9. Nancy Reagan
j. gentle	10. President Bush
k. authoritative	11. Elizabeth Taylor
l. healthy	12. Pope John Paul II
m. integrated	13. Mikhail Gorbachev
n. attractive	
o. compassionate	
p. ruthless	
q. controlling	

Part 2:
Match the people in column "B" with the feeling words in column "A". You may use more than one word from column "A" to describe a person.

"A"	"B"
a. compulsive	1. My Mom
b. fat	2. My Dad
c. isolated	3. My Brother
d. peaceful	4. My Sister
e. powerful	5. My Grandmother
f. thin	6. My Grandfather
g. powerless	7. My Aunt
h. domineering	8. My Uncle

i. loving
j. gentle
k. authoritative
l. healthy
m.integrated
n. attractive
o. compassionate
p. ruthless
q. controlling

9. My Son
10. My Daughter
11. My Spouse
12. My Sponsor
13. Myself

Part 3:
Match the person in column "B" with the feeling words in column "A". You may use more than one word from column "A".

-A-
a. compulsive
b. fat
c. isolated
d. peaceful
e. powerful
f. thin
g. powerless
h. domineering
i. loving
j. gentle
k. authoritative
l. healthy
m.integrated
n. attractive
o. compassionate
p. ruthless
q. controlling

-B-
1. God

Part 4:
What conclusions can you draw about your image of God from the above exercise?

Your image of God is very closely tied to images you have of others and yourself, especially your parents. Parents role model God for their children and that image carries through to adulthood.

"My image of God is of a judge deciding what I do right and what I do wrong," said one woman. "Yes, my parents were very strict with me. They still are," she added.

"My God is personal and caring at times and indifferent at others," said another. "My mother was always around and never failed to show me affection as I grew up, but my father scarcely knew I was alive."

One man saw himself as a non-communicator, so his image of God was of a stern grandfather figure with his mouth closed and no expression on his face.

Who Is Your God?
Any definition of God is at best presumptuous and lacking in completeness. What follows are some experiences of God that partially describe who God is for people.

Very often, for many compulsive eaters, God is

someone who doesn't care or who's never around. "God is someone who disappointed me the way my parents disappointed me," said one man. This attitude gives fuel to the disease. The woman quoted next expressed it this way: "Food is my God," she said. "My life revolves around food. There is nothing I wouldn't do for it."

For some, God may be like a spouse because they have a good relationship with their spouse. For others, God is like a friend who's always there in time of need. For such people, God is more tangible and real, the way a sponsor is real. They come to see God not just in other people, but also in themselves.

"My definition of God keeps changing," said one woman. "When I was a child, God was a vague, blob-like entity. 'Father' was the only concept of God that was put forth then. My father died when I was young so I had no concept of God as father. I could only relate to some Higher Power that somehow was connected to me."

Another said, "I heard once that God is like a spouse whose face is so close that when the first spouse cries, the other spouse feels the tears on his own cheek. That's how close God is to our pain!"

God's Will

This can be a thorny issue for many people because it can interfere with what they want. And what they want may not necessarily be what's best for them. It all boils down to the question of control or manipulation. Seeking God's will is part of the process of letting go. When you're in flow with God's will, everything else flows.

How do you know what God's will is for you? If what you are doing makes you more peaceful, more loving, more outgoing, then it's wise to assume that this is God's will.

"I'm just learning that God's will is not for God to punish me or get back at me in any way, shape or form," said one compulsive eater.

"To me, God's will is to wish the best for me, to want me to become the fullest me," said Paul. "That's what God meant for me to be and that's why things will be more peaceful and loving. If I try to stop this flow, I can't be me. I can't be the person I'm to be."

"It's God's will for me to be able to recognize and use the gifts I have to the best of my ability," said Vivian. "I'm a work of art. We're all a work of art and we work in co-creating with God."

God's Way With You

How does God work with you? Is it the same for everyone? One way to find out answers to these questions is to go back to past experiences where you recognized or somehow sensed the presence of God. Sometimes this is called a peak experience because it revealed a truth or an insight was gained, but it doesn't have to be a high. It can be a very ordinary event that produced a sense that God was there.

"I had a peak experience four years ago," said one woman. "I knew I was obese. I knew I was unfaithful to what I believed about God. Even the weather was against me by being a hot Sunday night in July. But I was in Church, in the last pew, trying to put in a few minutes of prayer time. I knew I couldn't pray. Who was I kidding? I hadn't prayed for years. Prayer was like punching a time clock for me. When my time was up, I pulled my card out and ran. But this time, something happened. As I sat, a solitary figure in that last row, I suddenly felt loved. I could feel the love traveling down the pews coming toward me. I was loved as I was. Don't ask me how it happened. I don't know. But I walked out changed. I was not the same person I was before."

One man shared what happened to him as a passenger on a plane that was experiencing engine trouble and was losing altitude fast. "So many things flashed through my mind," he said. "All of a sudden I was telling God how to manage the plane. Then I realized there was nothing I could do but surrender to God. I saw God standing there waiting for me should I die and knew that I was safe with God even in death. I could go through this experience because God was there with me."

A third person said, "I had just finished dressing and was tying my shoes, a morning ritual I haven't varied for years, when I reflected on how much I thrive on the familiar rather than the unknown. I saw how important it is for me to know what to expect -- to have all the facts ahead of time -- in any given occurence and how much I freeze or am uncomfortable when I don't. Then I thought of dying. I can't know in advance what to expect of that situation! I laughed nervously, but I didn't panic, because instantly I sensed the presence of God telling me I would not be alone. I felt God present. I would be safe, and it would be OK even though I'd be traveling in unfamiliar territory."

Exercise 59
Think of a time when you were aware of God's presence in your life. Describe that below.

How Do You Pray?
How do you tell God what's in your heart? How do you hear what God is saying to you? What are the components of prayer and how do you do it?

Prayer is the act of bringing the truth of who you are into the reality of who God is. When this is distorted, so is prayer.

One woman recently complained of having a struggle with prayer. She said she thought she didn't know what she was doing. She felt like such a baby at prayer. Last year it had been so different, so easy. Then she was having problems coping with her mother's illness and eventual death, so her relationship with God was wonderful. Prayer was a snap. She was confident of God's presence. "We were communicating. We were on the same wavelength. I want some of that back today but without the crisis," she explained.

How do you find God so that you can pray? Another definition of prayer is that prayer is the *lowering* of the mind and heart to God because God resides within. This story from *The Song Of The Bird* by Anthony deMello illustrates the point clearly:

> "Excuse me," said an ocean fish. "You are older than I, so can you tell me where to find this thing they call the ocean?"
>
> "The ocean," said the older fish, "is the thing you are in now."
>
> "Oh, this? But this is water. What I'm seeking is the ocean," said the fish. And he swam away to search elsewhere.

What do you say to God in prayer? The same things you'd say to a good friend who loves you, for instance: what's happening to you, how you feel, the pain or crisis you're in.

"But I don't know how to pray," said one compulsive eater."

"Just get on your knees and say, 'God, please come into my life,'" said another. "I've done it over and over and my life has changed. I don't know who's coming, but it's something good."

Exercise 60
On a separate sheet of paper write a letter to God.

Exercise 61
Take a walk of thanksgiving through your own giftedness. Meditate on your own gifts, seeing what they are, and how you use them, thanking God for them. Write a short summary of your meditation experience below.

Exercise 62
What names do you call God by? What names does God call you by? Write them below.

Jot down what you are feeling right now.

Epilogue
Becoming Your Own Person

"It's incredible to me to feel alive, enthusiastic
and excited, and remember how I was
a short while ago."

Be A Co-Creator With God

If you've read the previous chapters and have identified with them, if you've done the exercises faithfully and discovered much about yourself and the disease, if you've chosen to exercise your right of choice and to be responsible for yourself in your recovery, then you have already started to become your own person.

By now you've come to realize you have a disease that is multi-faceted and all-encompassing. You know how to recognize and accept your feelings, how to be honest with them and how to express them appropriately. You've seen through control's deceptive face and accept that true control lies in doing all you humanly can and then "letting go" and trusting in the outcome. You've set boundaries that serve you in your recovery process of empowerment. Forgiveness and God have or will become a part of your vocabulary.

Now what? Are you cured? Is it over?

Hardly. A long road lies ahead. To tell you it's quick and easy would be to mislead you.

But don't despair, it isn't all hard. Like

everything meaningful in life, sometimes it will be easy and seem like no work at all. Other times, it will be harder.

Yet, you haven't stood still throughout this time, either. You've armed yourself the way a firefighter does before responding to a fire. Would you expect a firefighter to plunge into the heat of a burning building without the proper equipment and knowledge of what to do? Would you expect a doctor to practice medicine without some form of medical training and practicum experience? So you too have needed to know what to do and how to do it, practicing in bits and pieces through self-revealing and empowering exercises.

A Life-Long Process

"This route is a life-long process," said one compulsive eater in recovery.

"I thought it would be easy. I thought I had a little weight problem. Now I see how deep it is," said another.

"This isn't something I would do for a day, a week, or a month. It's a decision I have to make every day of my life," said Vivian.

Whether your falter or succeed, the possibility of that first compulsive bite is there daily. Temptations to take it are there every moment, but so is the choice. That's what you have to return to. So, this program, this philosophy, this way of being is not a diet that someday ends. It is a recovery process that is sometimes easy, sometimes hard, but definitely a life-long commitment that is to be worked at daily.

Living The Moment

"Today is ten days of abstinence for me. I'm willing to live for this day only. I'm willing not to freak out by looking at myself in the mirror, by being alone with myself. I'm willing to stop giving so much control to my food. I'm willing to go to meetings and to live with the program," said one woman.

"Recently, I went through a four-month depression. It was very scary. I don't want to go back there. I know I have to live for the moment," said a recovering bulimic.

"I take one day at a time," said Paul.

The Support Of The OA Fellowship

In becoming your own person, you're going to need some kind of support system and working tools to keep growing and changing. The OA Fellowship with its meetings available daily throughout almost every area of the country is the fertile soil in which to grow. OA meeting times and locations can be learned by calling your local chapter of Overeaters Anonymous listed in the white pages of your telephone book.

OA offers you the tools to build and maintain a successful program of recovery. The tools consist of observing and complying with the following practices: abstinence, anonymity, sponsorship, literature, meetings, telephone and service.

Abstinence is best defined as refraining from eating compulsively. This can mean a number of things. For some, it means staying away from their binge foods. For others, it means eating three healthy meals a day. It can also mean staying away from negative feelings. "Abstinence is the most important thing in my life. I'm willing to do whatever it takes," said a bulimic.

The use of **sponsors** is one of the characteristics that makes OA unique. A sponsor is a person who can help you personally. This person usually is one who has a program you like and who is willing to share his or her strength, hope and experience with you. This person is on the same level as you, perhaps with only a day, week, month, or year's worth more experience than you. Your sponsor is the person you call or visit when you are in need. "My sponsor showed me the light," said one compulsive eater.

Anonymity provides confidentiality and protects everyone's rights to feel free and safe and trusting. No last names are used at the meetings, only first names, and sometimes even nicknames. The leveler here is the disease and members are seen and treated as equal rather than different from each other.

The *telephone* is the way to link up with other members when help is needed, especially when the need is immediate. The phone call is a mini-meeting with someone who can offer clarity, direction and support. "When I call my sponsor, I'm more willing to say how I feel," said one man.

"The loneliest place in my house is my kitchen. The telephone can be a true lifesaver," said Vivian.

Service involves such tasks as taking people to OA meetings, setting up the chairs once there, making coffee, or leading the meeting. "You can only keep the program by giving it away," said one man.

"The most important service you can do is to take yourself to a meeting," said Paul.

Literature pertains to the reading of supportive materials such as the Big Book of AA, the 12 Steps and 12 Traditions of AA for whatever length of time you have available. "If I'm feeling crazy, I know it's time to take a one minute meditation," said one woman.

Meetings refer to all types of OA meetings, for example, closed discussion meetings, open meetings, step meetings, and beginners meetings.

Unfolding Your Life's Issues

In becoming your own person, you'll re-examine or possibly examine for the first time all your life's issues. Who Am I? What past life events, people or forces shaped me? What is life? How can I be happy? What is success and where can I find it? One man in recovery recently said, "Success is failure turned inside out."

Other questions you may ask yourself are: Does my job really fulfill me? Am I using my gifts and talents to the best of my ability? How can I improve my work life? Should I apply for another type job, or at another place?

Awareness of all these issues allows for choice. Whenever choice is not denied, the unpleasantness or limitations of any situation is diminished. "When I chose to ask my mother for advice on certain matters, I didn't mind her telling me what to do. But when I had to listen to her advice without asking for it or needing it, it became an intrusion into my life," said one man.

"PAT" -- Pray, Act, Trust

Compulsive people so often think in black and white, in only one way, with no options. Not so with the recovering person. A recovering person remembers and practices PAT. PAT stands for Pray, Do Appropriate Action, and Trust as a way of living.

"I pray that I may surrender to God all my limitations, concerns and fears. I ask for guidance and wisdom to know what the best thing to do is when I am faced with a problem," said one man.

"Along with my time of prayer, I also check with others I trust so that I can discern what appropriate action or actions I can take in any given situation. Then I do it," added a woman.

"After this there's nothing left to do but to trust in God, in my actions, in others' response and in the outcome. In other words, to let go and let be," said another.

This is a wonderful way of staying open to life. It allows for a great deal of flexibility and the chance to develop a non-attached and therefore non-controlled view to life and all that life holds.

Other Helps Along The Way

During recovery, you'll be doing a great deal of reflection. The use of a journal where you can jot down and share your feelings and the day's events is very helpful. You don't want to isolate or you'll resort to the food as your only friend.

A healthy regime in life, such as exercise, is another help because it tones both mind and body. Choose some form of physical activity that you can do daily or almost daily. Walking is still the all-time favorite. Done alone or with a friend, a walk allows minds, hearts and limbs to be stretched and aired.

What Will You Do Now?

Do you recall the beginning of the book when Paul saw himself sitting on the fence? As long as he remained there he was torn between two opposing forces. One is food; the other, life. The former is addictive and destructive for him; the latter, freeing and productive.

Paul chose life. So did Vivian and countless others. All these people chose to empower themselves with the means to recover. They're doing it step by step, moment by moment, one day at a time.

Now that you've come this far, what will you do? Will you "chance" the disease by going back to it or will you choose life using the 12 Step program of OA and the OA fellowship support system to help you as you go along?

It's up to you. What will you do?

Jot down what you are feeling right now.

Glossary

Abstinence -- the act of voluntarily refraining from eating compulsively.

Addiction -- the act of habitually giving oneself over to or being under the power of any substance such as food, drugs, or alcohol; the compulsive and out-of-control use of any chemical substance which when discontinued can produce unpleasant, recognizable withdrawal symptoms.

Anger -- a feeling of distress resulting from perceived injury, mistreatment or opposition, usually showing itself with a desire to fight back in some form.

Anorexia -- a personality disorder, usually in young women, characterized by an aversion to food and an obsession with weight loss.

Attitude -- the position or posture assumed by the body or the mind in connection with an action, feeling, or mood.

Boundary -- any point, line or thing marking a limit or border.

Bulimia -- a continous, abnormal hunger.

Bulimic -- a person who purges through dieting, or

fasting, or excessive exercise, or laxatives or diuretics.

Co-dependent -- a person who knowingly or unknowingly has an inappropriate hold on another. Also a person who has lost his or her sense of self.

Communication -- the act of transmitting, giving, or exchanging of information, signals, or messages by talk, gestures, or writing.

Compulsion -- an irresistible, repeated, irrational impulse to perform some act.

Compulsive eater -- someone who cannot control the type and amount of food he or she consumes.

Control -- to regulate, direct, command or exercise authority over.

Eating disorder -- a condition resulting from eating or non-eating that interrupts or interferes with life.

Enabler -- someone who thinks he or she can do something about another's disease.

Feeling -- a natural, spontaneous reaction to something that one perceives as happening or not happening to oneself.

Forgiveness -- the act in which one ceases to blame others and ceases to feel resentment toward them.

OA Fellowship -- men and women who share their experiences, strengths and hopes with each other so that they may solve their common problem and help others to recover.

Obsession --an abnormal or irrational urge, something that haunts, troubles, or pre-occupies someone to a great degree.

Prayer --   the act of lowering the mind and heart to God who resides within.

Resentment -- a persistent feeling of bitter hurt and indignation from a sense of being injured or offended; anger that is re-felt and re-fueled.

Sponsor -- a person living in recovery who undertakes certain responsibilities to understand, advise, and promote the recovery of another.

The 12 Step Program -- the guiding force to living for all those in recovery from an addiction.

RECOMMENDED READING

-----<u>Alcoholics Anonymous,</u> World Services Inc., New
York City, 1986.

Beattie, M., <u>Codependent No More,</u> Hazelden
Foundation, Center City, Minnesota, 1987.

DeMello, Anthony, S.J., <u>One Minute Wisdom,</u>
Doubleday, 1986.

Hollis, J., <u>Fat Is A Family Affair,</u> Hazelden
Foundation, Center City, Minnesota, 1985.

-----<u>For Today,</u> Overeaters Anonymous Inc., World
Sevices Inc., New York City, 1982.

Jampolsky, Gerald G., M.D., <u>Love Is Letting Go Of
Fear,</u> Celestial Arts, Millbrae, California, 1979.

Nakken, Craig, <u>The Addictive Personality,
Understanding Compulsion In Our Lives,</u>
Harper/Hazelden, 1988.

-----<u>Overeaters Anonymous,</u> Overeaters Anonymous
Inc., World Services Inc.

Peck, Scott, <u>The Road Less Traveled,</u> Simon and
Schuster, New York, 1978.

Phelps, J. and A. Nourse, <u>The Hidden Addiction and</u>

How To Get Free, Little, Brown and Company, Boston, Massachusetts, 1986.

Roth, Geneen, Breaking Free From Compulsive Eating, Macmillan, New York, 1985.

Roth, Geneen, Feeding The Hungry Heart, McMillan, New York, 1982.

Schaef, Anne W., Co-Dependence Misunderstood, Mistreated, Harper & Roe, New York, 1986.

Sullivan, M. and R. M. Dunphy, "Compulsive Overeating In The Convent," Human Development, Fall 1989.

Viscott, David, M.D., The Language of Feelings, Morrow, New York, 1976.

OTHER RESOURCES
CO-DEPENDENTS ANONYMOUS
P.O. Box 33577, Phoenix, AZ 85067-3577
EMOTIONS ANONYMOUS
P.O. Box 4245, St. Paul, MN 55104
OVEREATERS ANONYMOUS
P.O. Box 92870, Los Angeles, CA 90009

Compulsive Eaters Retreats are given throughout the U.S. and Canada by Mary Sullivan, r. c. For a listing of these retreats or the one nearest you, write or call:

Mary Sullivan, r.c.
1400 S. Dixie Highway
Lantana, Florida 33462   Tel. # 407-582-2534